1001
WAYS OF
SAVING MONEY

TONY SWINDELLS

David & Charles
Newton Abbot – London – Vancouver

To
Duncan

ABOUT THE AUTHOR

Tony Swindells spent 20 years in advertising, mostly with agencies, before becoming a full-time lecturer. He is now the tutor for two courses in advertising at Watford College of Technology. He has previously had published a text book, *Advertising Media & Campaign Planning* (Butterworths, 1966).

British Library Cataloguing in Publication Data

Swindells, Tony
    1001 ways of saving money. – ('Mirror' books).
    1. Finance, Personal – Handbooks, manuals, etc.
    I. Title II. One thousand and one ways of saving
    money III. Series
    332'.024   HG179
    ISBN 0–7153–7540–7

First published by Mirror Books Ltd 1976
This David & Charles edition 1978

© Mirror Books Ltd 1976

Printed in Great Britain
by A. Wheaton & Co Ltd, Exeter
for David & Charles (Publishers) Limited
Brunel House Newton Abbot Devon

Published in Canada
by Douglas David & Charles Limited
1875 Welch Street North Vancouver BC

CONTENTS

INTRODUCTION

Today, we British are united behind one idea as never before. Regardless of all other differences, we all share the same unshakable belief: that we're hard up.

So, what can we do about it? What with increasing prices, devaluing cash, the ever hungry tax man and the frequent wage freezes or limits on pay increases, it seems that only two options remain: we can emigrate – or we can economise until things get better. This book is intended to help all those who decide to soldier on.

First, though, let's rid the book of the ambiguity in its title. By 'saving money' we mean *economising* – using money sparingly and turning it to the best account – *not* merely piling it up.

Basically, there are only five ways of saving: by buying more cheaply, by buying less often, by eliminating waste, by doing/making/growing it yourself and by going without. Most of these methods hurt a little, because they mean that something has to be sacrificed – usually convenience, speed or comfort. Living in a consumer-orientated society, we have all taken these for granted in the past. Now we must relinquish some convenience, speed and comfort for a while.

But there is one valuable compensation for scrimpers: the feeling that they are winning their own financial battles and doing so in a deflationary way – a way which will help the country. And if that sounds like an exaggeration, consider that there are over $18\frac{1}{2}$ million households in Britain – each one of them, almost certainly, needing to economise. Most of them, of course, are now resigned to having to make savings. What they lack, however, is the know-how. This book meets that need.

Here, covering 15 areas of expenditure, you will find tips of all kinds – some old, some new, some resulting in considerable savings, others in only marginal economies. But don't despise the small savings; they soon mount up if made regularly. Find a way of saving 2p per day, every day, and you will save £7.30 in one year.

Of course, some of the suggestions will appeal to you more than others. However, with such a large choice, everyone should be able to find several suitable economies which, at the very least, will save many times the cost of this book.

Tony Swindells

How to save money on
Babies & Children

1 Baby clothes (1)
Pause before spending money on baby clothes. You will probably be given many items by friends and relatives. Avoid duplication by waiting for all the presents to arrive. With luck, there may not be much that has to be bought. When you do buy, choose neutral colours, like primrose, peach or green, so that the items may be used again for future offspring, as yet unscheduled. Do not turn up your nose at second-hand baby clothes — often these are as good as new, and much cheaper.

2 Baby clothes (2)
All-in-one stretch suits are real money-savers during baby's first three months (possibly longer, depending on size at birth). Three suits should see baby through this time (one to wear, one spare and one in the wash). Made in stretch cotton/nylon terry, these garments expand as the baby gets bigger. They save expense on gloves, mittens and nighties.

3 Baby foods – home-made
A liquidiser is a money-saving investment when baby is able to take solids. It enables you to blend your own baby foods. Thus, he can eat much the same foods as the rest of the family instead of all those little tins of goo.

4 Baby foods – instant
Instant powdered baby foods are much more economical than tinned ones because, when baby is eating only two or three teaspoonsful per meal, you can mix exactly the right amount for him.

5 Baby – having a: information
When a woman is going to have a baby, it is natural for her to want as much information as possible. She could

spend a small fortune upon the many reference books. Or she can get everything she needs from two free booklets published by the British Medical Association: *You & Your Baby* (i) *From Pregnancy to Birth* and (ii) *From Birth to Two Years.*

Enquire at your local ante-natal clinic about these or similar books.

The public library is another free source.

6 Baby linen
Never buy baby-sized bed linen. Get blankets and sheets big enough for a child's bed and double them over. Baby will become a toddler and then a school child quicker than you may think.

7 Baby's cotton wool
Balls of cotton wool for baby's toilet are an expensive buy when you consider that a roll of cotton wool is (proportionately) much cheaper and, with the aid of an orange stick and a little patience, will provide hundreds of such balls – or you can simply tear off small wads as you need them.

8 Baby-sitting
Why pay out cash for baby-sitters when you can start a baby-sitting group with your friends and neighbours? Each member of the group takes it in turn to 'keep the book' for, say, a month. During that time, the holder of the book receives requests for sitters, finds out who is available, and keeps account of the time given by group members. The idea is to 'pay' for your own baby-sitter, not in cash, but by sitting the same amount of time for someone else.

9 Baby's nappies
Babies need nappies for about two years. If you buy disposables, it is estimated that two years' supply will cost about £60. If you buy the traditional towelling squares, you will need two dozen and they will cost about £12. It is true that, if you wash the nappies the 'normal' way, you will use much expensive hot water – but this need not be. Just give the soiled nappy a quick whirl under the cold water tap and then soak in a solution of cold water and one of the branded germicidal nappy cleansers. This way nappies may be easily hand washed without troubling the washing machine.

Baby stain remover
See no. 764, 'Puppy/baby stain remover'.

10   Baby's underpants
When baby gets too big and sophisticated for nappies, you are left with a great pile of the things, wondering how to use them (unless, of course, you plan another baby later on). One way is to dye them and use as hand-towels, but who needs two dozen hand-towels? Another way is to turn them into elastic-topped toddler underpants.

11   Baby toiletries
There is a natural motherly tendency to lavish jellies, creams, oils, perfumes and powders of all sorts upon one's progeny. If you can resist this urge and make do with cotton wool, *Bath Care* (which serves as both soap and shampoo), petroleum jelly (to prevent nappy rash), talcum powder, a brush and comb – you will save money. (A large tub of petroleum jelly may last up to a year.)

12   Books – children's
Most children receive two or more annuals for Christmas. These books, which are not cheap, are often discarded after only one reading. If you have a number of friends, relatives and neighbours with children of about the same age, why not agree to buy one book each (making sure that no two families buy the same book) and then swop around? In this way, each child sees more annuals at less cost to the parents.

13   Clothing – children's (1)
Children grow out of their clothes at a ruinous rate, so that parents soon acquire masses of nearly new – but redundant – clothing. Most people either keep them for future children or pass them on. In the same way as for the books (see no. 30), the passing on process can be greatly improved and accelerated by the formation of a group. If, say, ten families on an estate (or with children at the same play group) all join in, the clothing can be recycled rapidly to everyone's benefit. There need be no fuss, no rules, no exchanges. By wearing the clothes to destruction, expenditure on new clothing is greatly reduced.

14   Clothing – children's (2)
When buying for children, always get the next size larger.

15 Cradle

Don't spend money on a cradle. A laundry basket or a deep drawer (suitably lined – and removed from its chest, of course) makes an adequate cradle for baby's first few months.

16 Glove puppets

Children love glove puppets – and anybody with an old, worn out sock and a needlework basket can make one. Just stitch a nose in the centre of the toe, add two buttons for eyes and two pieces of material for ears – and you have produced a potential star of stage, screen and television!

17 Name-tapes

If you have two or more children who *must* have printed name-tapes for their clothing (and some schools do insist), there is a way to reduce printing costs. In the case of two children, order the tapes to be printed with one child's initial, followed by the surname, followed by the other child's initial, all on one tape, thus: A ROBINSON W. Then, cut off the initial not wanted in each case. If you have three children at the school, get the tape printed A B ROBINSON W. You then cut off the A and W to leave B ROBINSON, or cut off the A B to leave W. But to make tapes for A ROBINSON, you need to cut off the B and the W, which would leave the tape in two pieces. Stick both parts down on to sticky tape before sewing to the clothing.

18 Paste – children's

The water left over from boiling rice or potatoes is full of starch. If thickened by extra boiling, this makes a reasonable paste for use in a child's scrapbook.

19 Pictures for the wall of a child's room

Some of the gift wrapping paper sold today is so decorative and/or informative that it is well worth a place on the wall, thus providing a very colourful 'chart' or 'montage' for a fraction of the price of the real thing. (For ironing used gift paper see no. 47.)

20 Plasticine substitute

Make your own modelling dough. Mix together $1\frac{1}{2}$ cups plain flour, $\frac{1}{2}$ cup water, 2 tablespoons of cooking oil and 1 cup salt. Add food colouring, if you wish.

21 Pram
The large, old-fashioned pram is something of a luxury in these days of the much more convenient (and cheaper) carry-cot and transporter. Resist the temptation to keep up with the Joneses – and save the money.

22 Playthings – children's
Bazaars, charity fairs and jumble sales are good sources of cut-price playthings, especially books, toys and jig-saw puzzles. For example, a bundle of comics may be picked up for as little as 2p at a jumble sale.

23 Pyjama trousers – children's
When pyjama legs become too short, cut them off at the knees, and re-hem leaving Bermuda-type pyjama shorts for summer wear.

24 School clothing
The School Shop, Yorkshire House, Shambles Street, Barnsley, Yorkshire, is well worth investigation. Send for their mail order catalogue: you may well find that they stock your child's uniform at a much cheaper price than you would pay locally. Although you would need to add the badges yourself.

The Young Idea catalogue lists children's clothes from birth to 13 years and includes school wear. For a copy of their catalogue, write to: *Young Idea Ltd., Kingsbury, Aylesbury, Bucks.*

25 Scrap/drawing books
Scrap and drawing books for children are expensive – and rarely last very long. You can make a cheaper, yet thicker, book by purchasing a roll of lining paper from a wallpaper shop and cutting it into sheets double the size of the finished page. Fold them in half and place between covers of hardboard or thick card which have been hinged to each other by carpet tape or glued canvas. Now run a piece of string along the centre fold and around to the back of the tape-hinge. Tie string ends together.

26 Toys (1)
Every experienced parent knows that the most expensive toys are very often the ones which junior chooses to ignore. If you find yourself playing with one of these (while your child shows more interest in the cardboard

container), look around for another parent playing with an expensive toy and do a swop.

When choosing or (better) making toys, it is wise to remember that children enjoy *doing* – not watching. A motorless train that has to be pushed around the track by hand is far more interesting to young children than a boring motorised one which keeps going round by itself. Simple, home-made toys fashioned from boxes, tins, cotton-reels, tubes, haricot beans and plastic containers can give enormous pleasure.

27 Toys (2)
Any problems or queries concerning British-made toys will be dealt with by: *The British Toy Manufacturers' Association Ltd., Regent House, 89 Kingsway, London WC2 6PS (01–242 9158).*

How to save money on
Celebrations & Entertainment

28 Birthday cards
Buy reasonably priced birthday cards throughout the year, whenever you see really good ones. If you wait until a few days before the date, the chances are that the shop will not have anything suitable at the right price and you will be forced to buy a more expensive card.

29 Birthday presents
If any of your friends have birthdays early in the year, it is worth remembering that, immediately after Christmas, most large stores sell off boxes of liqueur chocolates at half price. Sometimes these are clad in Christmas cartons, but often they will have plain cartons underneath.

30 Book club
If, in your circle of friends, there are a few of you who enjoy reading more or less the same type of novel or paperback, why not form your own book club? You need to meet at regular intervals — say, once a month — and to decide which book each of you will buy. Then circulate them on a rota basis. The same idea may be applied to records, sewing patterns or even children's toys.

31 Cake board
Don't buy one. Instead, measure the diameter of your cake, add 3", and cut a disc of that size from a piece of thick cardboard. Place circle on remaining cardboard, draw around it with a pencil and cut a second circle. Repeat to produce a third — or even a fourth — circle. Place them on top of each other, gluing together or fastening with sticky tape around the edges. Cover completely with a sheet of tinfoil and secure underneath with either sticky tape or a dab of rubber glue.

32 Cake decoration

You know how it is when you decorate a cake with royal icing – you always make too much because you are afraid of not having enough. Instead of throwing away the surplus, or giving it to the children, pipe flowers and stars on to a sheet of waxed paper, leave to dry, then store in a tin, ready to decorate another cake or trifle.

33 Christmas cards (1)

If yours is one of two or more related households which send several Christmas cards to one another, why not call a truce and agree not to send any (providing the bonds of friendship are sufficiently strong). After all, it's the thought that counts. (Warning: Unless you wish to lose your friends, don't try it with birthdays.)

34 Christmas cards (2)

Home-made Christmas cards are considerably cheaper – and they are valued much more by the recipients. A few red, blue or yellow cards, pieces of white or coloured paper from which to cut Christmas tree or snowman shapes, tinsel, glue and a little imagination can produce cards as good as the ones in the shops. (If you have no artistic streak and feel that your efforts may be frowned upon, get the children to make the cards. This way they will be very acceptable and probably more treasured.)

35 Christmas decorations

One of the most attractive Christmas tree decorations is very easy to make. Simply cut stars of different sizes from cardboard, cover them in coloured tinfoil and hang with thread. Painted egg-shells and fir cones also look effective.

36 Christmas/Easter gifts

Christmas/Easter wouldn't be the same without gifts. And when the members of two or more households exchange gifts annually, there is a tendency for those gifts to become a little grander, year by year. Thus, even without any help from inflation, we tend to spend more and more in this way. Add inflation, and the amount of money that a family gives away in the form of seasonal presents can be ridiculous. Seasonal extravagance makes no sort of sense if the housewife has to skimp for the rest of the year. The best way around this problem is for the families to put their heads together during the summer and agree upon a top limit to the cost of presents (and also a limit to their number). Doing this in no way spoils the fun. In fact, a price limit forces the giver to consider more carefully the tastes of the recipient, and will result in better chosen, more interesting gifts.

37   Christmas gifts (1)
The cheapest time to buy Christmas presents is during the July sales. This is one instance where forward planning certainly pays off.

38   Christmas gifts (2)
A particularly thoughtful (and therefore much appreciated) Christmas present may be made for hardly any cost, if you are prepared to spend the time. Immediately after Christmas, buy a cheap scrap book. During the next 12 months, cut out of newspapers and magazines every snippet you can find on the favourite topic of the one for whom you are making the gift. As Christmas draws near, sort through the items, arrange them attractively and paste them into the book. Subjects like knitting patterns, nature notes, gardening hints, pop groups or a particular football team are easy to collect and will be of absorbing interest to somebody or other.

39   Christmas poultry
Poultry is at its most expensive in Christmas week, so save money by buying early and freezing.

40   Christmas tree bauble fastener
Don't waste money on fancy tape – the tags that secure plastic bread bags make very effective fasteners for Christmas tree baubles.

41   Colour TV
You can get colour TV for about £40 for a 25″ screen if you purchase an ex-rental set. They are advertised in the electronics magazines. Furthermore, when its cathode ray tube flickers no more, you can sell the body to radio enthusiasts, who will give you up to £20 for its components.

42   Drinks
Drinkers can save money either by switching to cheaper poison or by drinking less. If you are a beer drinker, try one of those home-brew kits. If you like the taste – and many converts claim that it is better than the watery fluid now sold as beer by public houses – you will save money.

43 Entertaining

There are times when close friends – say, three or four couples – would like to get together for a dinner party. Very often, however, they are prevented from doing so by the cost. The expense for one couple to entertain the others in this way would be considerable. Even the cost of a restaurant meal, with each couple paying its own way, could be forbidding. One economical way around this problem is for each couple to provide one course of the meal, together with a bill. The bills are then totalled, divided by the number of couples and the cost adjustments made as necessary.

44 Entertainment

Many people these days live not very far from a TV or radio studio. They all need studio audiences for the recording of their comedy, light entertainment, pop music and quiz programmes, and they all give free tickets. An evening in the studio can be much more interesting than the cinema or theatre. Programmes which you would not bother to switch on at home can be absorbing when you are actually taking part in the production of them. Phone the studio to explore the possibilities.

45 Gambling

Which type of gambler are you – once-a-week on the treble chance, or daily on the horses? If you are a pools person, you should realise that the odds against you getting eight draws in one line are several millions to one. With an average expenditure per week and average luck, you should hit the jackpot once every 400 years. There is another important fact which most treble chancers fail to understand: it is impossible to win a very large dividend by following form. The trouble is that several million other people who are also following the same form are bound to arrive at much the same answer as yourself. So, if results are true to form, you will all share the dividend. The only way to win a really big prize on the treble chance is by some entirely random method of selection – like using birthday numbers or the time-honoured jab with a pin – because these are the only ways that you are likely to produce a unique line. You really would stand a far better chance of winning something by buying premium bonds.

If you follow the horses because you like the daily excitement of battling against the odds, your money-saving methods could be: to stop altogether; to stop for a period of the year; to reduce your stakes; or to place fewer bets. You should certainly keep a record so that you know exactly how well/badly you are doing.

46 Gift paper (1)
Christmas wrapping paper is much cheaper in January. Buy it then and keep it in a safe place.

47 Gift paper (2)
Iron old gift paper with a medium hot iron on the unprinted side.

48 Gift paper (3)
The weekend colour supplements, women's magazines and TV weeklies sometimes have double pages printed in full colour and right up to the edge of the page (no white border). These make very acceptable gift wrapping paper.

49 Gifts – metal
Attractive desk tidies, flower-pot holders, waste bins, pastry cutters, flour scoops, lamps, children's toys and wall storage units for the kitchen may all be fashioned from empty food cans. Tools required to do this are a wall-mounted tin-opener, a junior hacksaw, a fine file, a light hammer, a large soldering iron, solder and flux, emery paper, a vice, drill bits and paint. The only other requirements are imagination and ingenuity. Don't forget that cans are made of tin-plated mild steel and can be very sharp when cut. Edges should be blunted by rubbing down with emery paper. Also, the cut edges should be re-tinned by coating them with melted solder (running the soldering iron around the exposed edge will do). This will prevent the steel going rusty.

50 Gift tags
Make gift tags by cutting old Christmas and birthday cards into small pictures.

51 Photographs
When taking films (other than transparency films) in to the chemist or photographic shop, ask for them to be 'developed only', which means you will receive only the negatives. You will be able to study these to decide from which ones you would like prints made. Alternatively (with black and white films), if you think you might find it difficult to judge the merits of your photography from

negatives alone, ask the assistant to 'develop and supply a contact strip'. This will be slightly dearer than 'develop only', but it will mean you will receive both the negatives and a strip of prints, all the same size as the negatives. From these you will be able to select the pictures you would like printed up to your 'regular' size.

52 Postage for greetings cards
If you must send several cards from one household to another, save the postage by putting them all in one envelope — or by including them with a gift.

53 Postage for presents
You can save postage on Christmas and birthday presents by a little forward thinking. Buy your presents (and cards) well in advance and deliver by hand the next time you visit or happen to be passing. Everybody enjoys receiving presents, even if they are not to be opened until months later.

54 Postcards/notelets
Expensive looking postcards can be made for nothing by cutting the message part off last year's Christmas and birthday cards. If this can be done so as to leave both the picture and the blank back page on the other side of the fold, the card may be used as a notelet.

55 Present
If you grow indoor plants, there will surely be times when a visitor enthuses over one or other of them. If it is someone to whom you normally give a Christmas or birthday present, make a note of which plant interested them, then pot a cutting for his/her Christmas present.

56 Radio
According to BBC's *Tomorrow's World*, a portable radio which costs 2p per unit of electricity when run off the mains, costs £7 per unit when run off batteries. *Must* your radio be mobile?

57 Smoking
Of course, we all know that every cigarette we smoke is both a health hazard and an expense, and the sensible thing would be never to smoke another. But it isn't so easy to stop, once you're hooked. If you are a no-hope, dyed-in-the-lung smoker, your best plan for saving money is, perhaps, to cut back a little. The first step is to work

out how much money per annum you are burning. Twenty per day at 50p is £182.50 per year. By cutting down by 10%, you could save £18.25 over the year. If you do decide on a 10% reduction, you now need to spread 18 cigarettes over the time which you normally take to smoke 20, which should not be too difficult.

58 Wedding receptions

The biggest expense at most weddings is the reception and the best way of economising on this is by not having a sit-down meal. You can achieve this decently and without losing face by having your reception at a time that would preclude a meal. For example, a two o'clock wedding could be followed by a reception with champagne, hot and cold buffet, wedding cake and coffee or tea.

How to save money on
Clothing
& Footwear

59 Clothes – all kinds of (1)

Many people have a real aversion to second-hand clothing, but, if you really want to save money on dress, the way to do so is by patronising the local jumble sale. It is possible to chop about 95% off your annual clothing bill in this way; but you must observe certain rules. Rule 1: Arrive well before opening time; there will certainly be a queue. Rule 2: Don't touch any of the underclothes – you have to draw the line somewhere. Rule 3: Likewise, don't touch the footwear – you don't know where they've been, and infections of the foot are far too common. Rule 4: Don't reject things simply on their face value. Remember, when you are paying only a few pence for a garment, you can afford to have alterations made. And some clothes are worth buying merely for their buttons, zips or belts! Rule 5: Although many of the clothes at jumble sales appear never to have been worn, it is advisable, for one's own peace of mind, for everything to go either into the washing machine or to the dry-cleaner's before you wear them.

60 Clothes – all kinds of (2)

Don't overlook the Government surplus shops when looking for really attractive bargains in clothing. Many garments cost only a fraction of the price you would expect to pay elsewhere. For example, superb woollen Naval pullovers at £1; an overcoat (priced in other shops at £40) for only £8.

61 Clothes/furnishings

People who make their own clothes and furnishings usually save more than half the shop price.

62 Cuff-links

Very decorative cuff-links can easily be made by connecting pairs of fancy buttons together with thread, leaving about 1½″ between the buttons. (The buttons should be the kind which have a ring at the back to take the thread, so that it is not visible from the front.) Also, make sure they are small enough to go through the shirt's button-holes. Pass many strands of thread backwards and forwards between the two buttons and then wind the remaining thread around the connecting strands to bind them into a string.

63 Dress – girl's

When making a dress for a growing girl, make it longer in the waist and machine in a tuck (instead of giving it a deep hem). Later, when the dress is lengthened, any sewing marks will be concealed by the belt.

64 Dressing gown/overcoat

If you've abandoned conventional bedding for the trendier continental quilts, you probably have chests full of blankets. Unless you wish to keep them (for visitors or extra-cold nights), why not dye them and buy a suitable paper pattern, which you can use to convert them into either dressing gowns or – if you are really clever – overcoats.

65 Dressmaking fabrics

Don't buy your material at the same time as your dressmaking pattern or you will almost .certainly waste money. Buy the pattern first. Take it home and experiment with it to find the most economical layout. Also, remember to check the hem length on the pattern against your own requirements. (Patterns allow for the wearer being tall; perhaps you are not.) By measuring up in this way before purchasing the material, you could save over a yard.

66 Fur coat cleaning

Cleaning your own fur coat will not produce as good a result as a professional furrier would achieve, but by doing it yourself from time to time you will save money because you will be spacing the professional cleanings further apart. Here's how it's done: Place an old blanket, doubled over, on a table, and cover it with a dust sheet. Place your fur on this. Now you need a bucket full of clean sawdust. Take a handful of this and rub it into the fur with a backwards/forwards movement, so that the sawdust particles scour the fur fibres. You must do every area of the coat systematically inch by inch. When completed, gather up the dust sheet with the sawdusted fur securely inside, take out of doors and thoroughly shake out all the sawdust. Next, take the fur back to your table and place it it on the blanket pad. You must now give it a gentle but thorough beating, preferably with a bamboo cane. If you do not possess a bamboo cane — and why should you? — use a springy garden cane (a clean one, of course). Finally, gently comb the fur against its natural grain. The hair will stand up fluffily. (Do not comb a naturally curly fur, like Persian lamb.) You can get your sawdust from a sawmill or timber yard and you will need about 2lb per coat.

67 Handbag
Many a handbag has been thrown out because its handle has broken. Next time you have a handle-less handbag, ask yourself how it would look with a gilt chain handle. If the answer is, 'fine', call at the ironmonger's to see if they stock suitable chains. In fact, they may do the whole job for you. If sewing is required, take the handbag and chain to a shoemender.

68 Inner soles
Remove the band from an old felt hat, hold the hat in the steam from a boiling kettle, then iron flat. You can now use the felt to make inner soles for slippers or shoes.

69 Jeans (1)
Buy jeans a few sizes too big, giving extra length. Cut this off (allowing a hem for possible shrinkage) and use it to patch the knees before the jeans have been worn. When the patches wear, as they surely will, take them off and replace with new ones.

70 Jeans (2)
When your jeans wear out, use them for patching your new ones.

71 Knitting wool (1)
You can prevent hand-knitted socks from shrinking or 'felting' by taking the following action before beginning to knit. Plunge the skeins of wool into very hot water and leave for about one minute. Pour off the water, squeeze

gently and hang up to dry before winding into balls.

72 Knitting wool (2)
Don't throw away old home-knitted garments. Unpick them. Wind the wool into skeins. Wash them in warm water. Keep flat while drying. Then re-knit.

73 Knitting wool (3)
Cut the cost of knitting an angora wool garment (without spoiling its appearance) by knitting each alternate row in ordinary two-ply wool of the same colour.

74 Knitting wool (4)
Don't be extravagant! Take longer over a garment by using a finer ply of wool and you will produce a much finer, cheaper woolly.

75 Maternity dress
You can make your own maternity gowns by adding a matching (or contrasting) panel, gathered or pleated, to the front of an ordinary dress.

76 Nylon stockings/tights (1)
If you would like your nylon stockings or tights to wear two or three times longer, here's what to do: Remove the dividers from your refrigerator's ice-cube tray. Place nylons in the tray and cover with water. Put tray in the freezer compartment and let the whole lot turn solid. After a few hours in this state, remove the tray from the refrigerator and allow to thaw gradually. Take out your nylons and allow them to dry slowly.

77 Nylon stockings/tights (2)
To lessen the risk of laddering, wear a pair of gloves when putting on or taking off your nylons or tights.

78 Nylon stockings/tights (3)
You have several nylon stockings of different shades? Boil them together in soapy water and they will all become the same shade.

79 Pullovers
When the long sleeves of a man's sweater wear thin, cut them off, bind the armholes and re-cycle as a sleeveless pullover.

80 Pullovers and cardigans
When a pullover or cardigan begins to wear at the

elbows, take out the sleeves and change them over. The thin wool will then be on the _inside_ of the arms.

81 Pyjamas
If you wear only half of your pyjama suit, why buy the other half? Barkers Bargain Basement sell jackets and trousers separately. Write them for prices, sizes and styles. They will sell by mail order. The address: _Barkers Bargain Basement, P.O. Box 21, Kensington High Street, London W8 5SE._

82 Pyjama top
When a shirt becomes worn at the collar and cuffs, remove the collar and shorten the sleeves. Also, remove the shirt lap (if it has one), making the lower edge of the garment even all the way round. Remove all the buttons except the top one and stitch up the front, leaving just enough of a gap for the head to pass through. Neatly re-stitch the neck band. Result: one Asiatic type pyjama top. (Wear with either conventional pyjama trousers or a sarong.)

83 Rubber boots
Preserve rubber boots or Wellingtons by rubbing them down with glycerine from time to time.

84 Shine remover
The shine on a dark suit can be removed by rubbing it gently with a rag soaked in spirits of turpentine. Alternatively, sponge with a mixture of one part vinegar to four parts water.

85 Shirt buttons
Even shirt buttons are expensive: why waste them? The next time you sew a button on a shirt, dab a little nail varnish (colourless, of course) in the centre of the button. It will seal the thread and prevent it from snapping.

86 Shoe repairs
The cost of shoe repairs these days is quite frightening, and shoes wear out as quickly as ever. So there is a very strong case for putting stick-on soles on to a new pair of shoes. It is best to wear the shoes a few times first, for a rougher surface will provide a better key for the adhesive. Metal heel and toe tips will lengthen the life of your shoes.

87 Shoes (1)
Buying cheap shoes is a waste of money because they do not last. It's much more economical to wait for the sales and buy two or three pairs of the very best quality you can afford. If worn in rotation – never the same pair on two successive days – they should last for several years.

88 Shoes (2)
One way to get the maximum value out of shoe sales is to ignore colour completely and concentrate upon quality, style, good fit and value for money. Once you have purchased your 'bargains', dye the shoes to the required colour – but be sure to use a good quality dye; some cheap dyes flake off after a short time.

89 Shoes (3)
An old hot water-bottle may be cut up to make soles and heels for Wellingtons or rubber over-shoes. For the bonding, use one of the toughest of the rubber (or all-purpose) adhesives.

90 Shoes and carpets
People who remove their shoes and wear carpet slippers upon arriving home not only reduce carpet wear – they also save shoe leather.

91 Sock – darning (1)
Mending socks can be a problem if you haven't any spare matching wool. You can unravel that problem by unravelling the wool – from the top of the sock. Oversew the top edge.

92 Sock – darning (2)
When darning socks, it is worth the extra trouble to feed a strand of thread through the eye of the darning needle, alongside the strand of wool. The extra strength will mean that the darn will last much longer, thus putting off the day when finally you have to fork out for a new pair of socks.

93 Socks – men's and children's
Men's and children's socks usually wear first at the heel or toes. You can delay this by rubbing the heels and toes with either soap or a wax candle after washing. The socks will last even longer if worn alternately on right and left feet, as this slows down the wearing action of the big toe.

94 Suede jacket

You can save money by spacing your suede jacket's visits to the cleaners further apart. Next time you're having a bath, hang the coat in the steam-filled bathroom for half an hour. Leave to dry. Brush with suede brush.

If you *must* have your suede (or sheepskin) garments dry-cleaned professionally, do not sign away your rights to compensation in the event of anything disastrous happening during the cleaning process – for in this way you could be signing away your money. Instead, look around for a cleaner displaying a guarantee card of the London Suede and Fur Cleaning Company. Such a cleaner will pay customers the full price of a replacement garment, should their own be spoilt. If you cannot find a local cleaner with one of these cards, write to: *LSFCC, 402 Green Lanes, Palmers Green, London N.13*. They operate a postal service for no extra charge.

95 Suit reviver

Put one teaspoon of household ammonia in one pint of warm water. Use a soft cloth or a cellulose sponge dipped into the solution to freshen up a tired looking suit. Hang it up in the open air so that the smell of ammonia will pass quickly.

96 Tights

Ladies, always buy tights of the same shade. Then, when a hole or ladder has appeared in one leg of each of two pairs, amputate the damaged limbs where they join the panties. Now you can wear both panties – one over the other – and each with one good leg.

97 Trouser turnups

Sometimes the backs of trouser turnups are the first parts to become frayed because they catch on the backs of the shoes. This can be avoided by sewing two small trouser buttons about $\frac{1}{2}''$ from the bottom of each trouser leg, on the insides.

98 Woolly jumpers

Old Shetland wool jumpers may be rejuvenated by adding a little cheap hair conditioner to the rinsing water after washing.

99 Woolly pullovers

It's a good idea to start knitting pullover sleeves from

the top, so that, when the elbows wear out or the sleeves need lengthening, it is easy to extend them.

100 Woollen socks

Woollen socks have a wasteful way of shrinking into uselessness. Prevent this by making two cardboard feet, slightly larger than the sock size, and placing them in the wet feet of the socks immediately after washing. Remove when socks are dry.

101 Zip protection

Before dumping clothes into the washing machine, make sure that all zips are zipped shut — and you will be less likely to have trouble with them later.

How to save money on
Cosmetics & Toiletries

102 Astringent lotion (1)
You can't beat witch-hazel (bought neat from the chemist) for a good, cheap astringent. But it is quite strong, so don't let it get into the eyes. Keep in the fridge and use ice-cold. It is antiseptic and reduces puffiness under the eyes. If you have small, suicidal children who are always falling on their heads, it is absolutely indispensable. Whacked on smartly, soon after the accident, it will prevent swelling.

103 Astringent lotion (2)
If you want a more 'fancy' astringent, like the ones you normally buy, try this. You will need: 1 peeled cucumber; 1 teaspoon witch-hazel; 1 teaspoon rose water; 1 egg white (beaten); $\frac{1}{4}$ teaspoon honey; $\frac{1}{4}$ teaspoon yoghurt. Crush up the cucumber. Add rose water, witch-hazel and frothed-up egg white, honey and yoghurt. Mix thoroughly. Put in fridge for few hours before use. This is claimed to be an efficient skin toner, but it will not keep for long.

104 Astringent lotion for enlarged pores (1)
If you suffer from enlarged pores around the chin and nose, try bathing with a little borax in warm water.

105 Astringent lotion for enlarged pores (2)
Large pores may also be reduced by applying iced salt water twice a day. Massage the solution gently into the area, taking care not to irritate the skin. Rinse away. Pat dry. Apply a soothing baby oil and blot away any excess.

106 Astringent lotion for mildly greasy skin (1)
An astringent skin lotion for use immediately after washing can be made by mixing cider apple vinegar with an equal amount of water.

107 Astringent lotion for mildly greasy skin (2)
The small amount of egg white left in the shells can also be used as a facial astringent. But be careful not to irritate the skin when applying – egg white does not agree with everybody.

108 Bath oil substitute (1)
Some country folk say that there are few finer bath additives than dandelion leaves and stinging nettles! Dry a number of dandelion leaves and nettles (handled with gloves) thoroughly. Crumble into a large bowl and add three or four pints of scalding water. Steep for 20 minutes. Strain off the solids. The remaining liquid, poured into the bath, cleanses, relaxes and refreshes the body. Make anew each time.

109 Bath oil substitute (2)
Dried blackberry and raspberry leaves, crumbled into a large bowl and infused with three or four pints of scalding water, also make an excellent freshener for use in the bath.

110 Bath oil substitute (3)
Fill a muslin bag with two cups of bran. Swish the bag about in the bath and the water will give a feeling of smoothness to the entire body. The bag may also be used as a wash cloth to add a lustre to the skin.

111 Bath oil substitute (4)
Try a blend of dandelions, cowslips and any other wild herbs of your choice. Infuse in three or four pints of boiling water. Strain and add the liquid to your bathwater.

112 Bath perfume
Put rosemary, sage, lavender and crushed bay leaf into a muslin bag. Tie the mouth tightly. You now have a bath bouquet garni.

113 Cleansing hand cream
You can save most of the money you spend on hand cream by making your own. First pick some elder flowers. Remove the stalks. Half fill a 1-lb screw-top jar with petroleum jelly. Pack the rest of the jar with the elder flowers. Stand the jar to simmer in a pan of water or cook gently for some hours with the top resting lightly on the jar (*not* screwed down). While the mixture is still hot, strain through muslin and add a few drops of

lavender or some other perfume. Allow to cool. Bottle in small jars. This is excellent for the hands after rough work.

114 Cosmetics
Where possible, instead of buying the product, buy the refill — it sometimes costs only one fifth of the product price.

115 Cuticle remover/nail bleach
No need to buy cuticle remover or nail whitener if you have a few drops of lemon juice left over in the kitchen.

116 Cuticle softener
Olive oil is excellent for softening the cuticles.

117 Dandruff preventative
Try this traditional method: Wash hair regularly, twice per week. Always rinse thoroughly, then dry with a towel, massaging the scalp briskly. Mix equal amounts of eau-de-Cologne and rose water. Dampen a clean hairbrush in the mixture and brush hair briskly.

118 Dandruff treatment
Some country folk stand by this old remedy: Infuse nettle leaves in boiling water and leave to cool. Strain off solids and massage liquid into the scalp. You can do the same with parsley. Both are good remedies for dandruff.

119 Eye freshener (1)
Pads of cotton wool soaked in warm milk and laid on the lids will freshen the eyes.

120 Eye freshener (2)
Two slices of cucumber cut into almond shapes and rested upon a pair of tired eyes will soon revive them.

121 Eye make-up remover
Inexpensive baby oil removes eye make-up efficiently.

122 Face-pack
Raw egg white left on the face for 10–15 minutes can be very effective as a skin tightener. However, this doesn't agree with everybody, so apply with caution.

123 Freckle remover
Buttermilk is a time-honoured (and cheap) answer to freckles. Smooth in gently into the skin at bedtime.

124 Hair care
Girls, if you buy a wig *of the same colour as your natural hair*, it will more than pay for itself by decreasing your visits to the hairdresser.

125 Hair conditioner (1)
Dry rosemary leaves can be used to make an effective hair conditioner. Place one teaspoon of dried leaves in a jug and add one pint of boiling water. Wait until cool. Strain.

126 Hair conditioner (2)
Greasy hair can be conditioned by adding a little starch powder to the shampoo.

127 Hair cuts
These days you can buy quite cheaply a gadget for cutting your own hair. With present hairdressing prices so high, you would not need to use it many times to recoup its cost. And to save even more money, but requiring some skill and a strong nerve, a wife could cut her husband's hair.

128 Hair lightener
Natural blondes can try emphasising the fact with the help of camomile flowers. Boil $\frac{1}{2}$ oz of the flowers in one pint of water for 20 minutes. Allow to cool. Use as hair rinse.

129 Hair tonic
Few things are better for giving life to dull hair than coconut oil, which may be bought cheaply from the chemist.

130 Hair treatment (1)
If you are a brunette, pour boiling water over rosemary leaves to make an infusion. Allow to cool. Use as final rinse after shampoo. it will add lustre to your hair. Infused rosemary leaves have long been used as a hair tonic and eyebrow darkener. If you are a blonde, do the same thing, but using camomile; if you have black hair, use sage.

131 Hair treatment (2)
Some old sailors maintain that sea salt can prevent falling hair. Stir two heaped tablespoons of sea salt into one quart boiling water. Allow to cool. Massage a little into the scalp every day. Shampoo normally.

132 Hand cream for dry skin
Mix olive oil and salt into a paste. Rub well into hands.

133 Hand lotion (1)
When the bottle is 'empty', replace the cap, turn it upside down and leave until next needed. And again! And again!

134 Hand lotion (2)
Chapped hands may be soothed inexpensively by a mixture of glycerine and rose water.

135 Hand rinse to prevent chapping
Make a mixture of vinegar and water. Use this to rinse the hands after washing. It will prevent them from becoming too dried, chapped or irritated.

136 Hard skin remover
Make a small muslin bag and fill with sea salt. Rub this over the skin when you have a bath and it will remove hardened layers of dead tissue, giving the skin a fine texture. No soap is required when using this pad.

137 Lipstick
It pays to be miserly with lipstick stubs. Wait until you have several, then melt them in a dish over a pan of hot water. Blend together until you have a pleasant shade. Allow to cool. Pour into small pot(s). Leave to set. Use a lip brush (or child's paint brush) to apply.

138 Make-up remover
For removing make-up, few things are more effective – or less expensive – than a slice of raw potato.

139 Mascara
Is your mascara tube empty? Then put one or two drops of water in it. You'll be surprised how much mascara you can get from an 'empty' tube.

140 Moisturizing cream
Baby creams are a lot cheaper than cosmetic moisturizing cream – and if they're good enough for baby's skin, they should be good enough for yours. Similarly, baby lotion is good for removing make-up; and baby oil – just a few drops – does wonderful things for your bath.

141 Nail varnish
Old nail varnish can be used to the last drop by adding a touch of varnish remover.

142 Nail varnish remover
Add a few drops of castor oil to some pure acetone. You now have a perfectly good nail varnish remover which, unlike neat acetone, will not dry too harshly.

143 Perfume
Inexpensive eau-de-Cologne can be made into something much more interesting by pouring it into an empty perfume bottle and giving it a good shake.

144 Razor blades
Used razor blades can be sharpened to give more shaves by honing them gently from side to side against the inner surface of a glass tumbler.

145 Scent
If you can find a bath oil with a perfume which you like (and which is fairly strong) you can use it instead of scent — it's cheaper.

146 Shampoo (1)
To make a mild shampoo, you need: $\frac{1}{2}$ teaspoon soft soap; 3 drops olive oil; and $\frac{3}{4}$ cup warm water. Mix and use normally. When rinsing your hair, use warm water containing a pinch of baking powder.

147 Shampoo (2)
Place scraps of green soft soap in water and bring to the boil. Allow to cool. Add a drop or two of perfume and you have the same shampoo which many professional hair-dressers used on their customers during wartime.

148 Shampoo (3)
If you do buy a branded shampoo, try using a much smaller quantity for each wash. Shampoo is expensive and using too much of it can damage your hair as well as your pocket. It does not matter if you do not have a scalp full of thick foam. The lather may feel good, but it is not strictly necessary.

149 Shampoo for fine hair
Take 4 oz soapwort root, chop small and infuse for ten minutes in half pint boiled water. The result is a soft, soapy water which, if used instead of a second shampoo, not only saves soap but also adds body to fine hair.

150 Shaving soap
One of the cleanest shaven men I know uses only two

safety razor blades per annum (by honing them on a tumbler (see no. 144) – and no shaving soap. He puts hot water on his face to soften the bristles and then carefully shaves with his 'old-fashioned' safety razor. He maintains that the absence of soap makes the cleaning of his blade easier and adds to its life.

151   Skin cleanser (1)
Believe it or not, _purée_ of lemon or tomato is a good treatment for an oily skin.

152   Skin cleanser (2)
You can cleanse the skin – especially a sallow skin – from the inside and outside by using dandelions. Make a strong tea from dandelion roots and leaves. Drink half cup every day and also use it to wash the face.

153   Skin lotion
Infuse 20 poppy petals in one pint of boiling water. Leave to stand for ten minutes. Strain. Cool. Some country folk claim that the lotion softens the skin and prevents wrinkles.

154   Skin nourisher
It is said that yoghurt nourishes and improves the texture of the skin while also removing discolouration. Apply it lavishly to the face and neck. Leave for half an hour, dabbing on more from time to time. Rinse off with rose water.

155   Skin tonic (1)
Try a little fine oatmeal sprinkled on the washing water to make a fine skin toner. Said to be especially good for greasy skin.

156   Skin tonic (2)
For an inexpensive skin tonic and freshener, mix half cup of distilled extract of witch-hazel (obtainable from the chemist or health shop) with half pint of tap water and add one tablespoon of toilet water.

157   Skin treatment
Parsley tea is an age-old remedy for blotchy skin. You make it in exactly the same way as ordinary tea, but using chopped parsley instead of tea leaves.

158   Soap
Once out of its wrapping paper, soap hardens. And hard

soap lasts longer. So store it nude. (And *must* you buy wrapped soap anyway? The unwrapped stuff is cheaper.)

159 Teeth
It is said that infused sage whitens the teeth.

160 Toilet soap
Scraps of soggy soap may be used by putting them into the toe of an old nylon stocking, knotting it near the toe and cutting away the spare piece. Use the soap bag for washing the hands.

161 Toothpaste
When your toothpaste tube seems to be empty, it will sometimes produce another week's supply if you unroll it, cut off the base and squeeze it from the other end. And when you believe your toothpaste tube to be finally empty, just soak it in hot water for a few minutes, then squeeze.

162 Wrinkle remover (1)
Put ordinary milk on the eyelids to keep them smooth.

163 Wrinkle remover (2)
Cut some gauze into strips about 2″ long. Dip them into the unbeaten white of an egg. Place them on to the face across the direction of the lines or wrinkles. Smooth down flat and hold in position until the gauze is dry. Remove by damping with warm water. Repeat daily and the lines should lessen or disappear. However, if you have sensitive skin, it is best to avoid this method – or apply with caution.

How to save money on
Decorating
& D-I-Y

164   Architectural advice for building work
When seeking expert advice about building work, do not overlook the architectural consultant. Although not legally entitled to call himself an architect (because he does not have the necessary paper qualifications), he may be every bit as good – and he will certainly be a lot cheaper. (Architects are not allowed to lower their fees, but consultants can please themselves.) In a *Which?* survey, 'Professional Advice for Building Work' (November, 1972), the consultants came out very favourably and considerably less expensive.

165   Bead curtain
You can make a bead curtain on the cheap by threading 2″ lengths of uncooked macaroni on to fine string and alternating with coloured beads.

166   Bookshelves
Smart, modern bookshelves can be simply made by placing a painted wooden plank on to three piles of three or four ordinary house bricks – one pile of bricks at either end of the plank and one supporting the middle. Three more piles of bricks are then placed on top of the first plank (directly above the first piles of bricks) and a second plank is added on top – and so on. If the shelves are positioned in an alcove, they may be given greater stability by cutting them to fit snugly into the available space. A pleasing effect may be obtained by painting the bricks white and the shelves a deep colour to match your decor.

167   Bricks
Building something? If so, do you really need new bricks? You can buy perfectly good second-hand bricks for about 80% of the normal price from local demolition sites.

168 Carpet for the loo/bathroom/hall

Whenever you fit a carpet and have a few feet left over – keep it! Whenever any of your friends have carpets laid, scrounge the end cuts! Don't hesitate to accept small carpet samples from the trade! If you must, you can buy a bundle of carpet pieces from any carpet stores. When you have enough, cut all your bits into 4″ squares. Lay them down loose with the pile going in different directions, just to make sure they fit. When you are satisfied with the effect, turn them over and stick edge to edge by applying carpet-tape or glued canvas strips to the underside. Turn the carpet over and press the pieces firmly into position.

169 Carpets (1)

When carpeting your home, do not make the mistake of buying the same quality for the entire house. Some rooms take a much heavier pounding than others, so match the quality to the need. Hardest wearing quality for stair carpets and hall; medium to good quality for the living room; medium for the dining room; and 'economy' quality for the bedroom.

170 Carpets (2)

Carpet prices for the same make vary enormously from dealer to dealer. So get several quotations – and hunt out the bargains. But even the 'bargains' will not be cheap, so it is essential to be able to buy wisely. And for that you need the facts. All necessary information is available from the following:

The Tufted Carpet Manufacturers Association, 231 Lower Road, London SE16.

Federation of British Carpet Manufacturers, British Carpet Centre, Dorland House, 14–16 Lower Regent Street, London W1 (01-930 8711). (Publish a useful leaflet called *Choosing the Right Carpet.*)

Carpet Products Manager, International Wool Secretariat, Wool House, Carlton Gardens, London SW1 (01-930 7300). (Publish a booklet *The Heart of a Home is a Wool Carpet.*)

171 Carpets (3)

It's much cheaper, when having carpets fitted by professionals, to get as much done at one time as you can afford. If possible, have the whole house carpeted at one go, even though you need to scratch around for the money. This uses the labour far more economically. One big job is far less costly than several small ones.

172 Carpeting tiles

Carpet tiles are very economical because of their absence of wastage. For example, you could start with a square of tiles in the centre of a room, adding around the edges as more money became available, and continuing until you had a fitted carpet effect. Further, if a tile is damaged, you simply take it up and replace. And you can change the floor pattern when you become tired of it by taking up some tiles and replacing with those of a different shade or colour.

173 Ceiling – binding and flaking

To cure flaking ceilings do not go to the expense of re-decoration. Instead, mix alum and water in the ratio of 1 oz to a quart. Wash the ceiling all over with this mixture, which will both bind and whiten its surface.

174 Curtains

Second-hand curtains bought at auction sales can be very good bargains. If you buy material at the sales, look out for items which have been drastically reduced in price because of negligible faults in the material. When buying a curtain material, it is a good long-term plan to choose one which later can be cut up to make loose covers.

175 Decorating

Bright, trendy colour schemes are more expensive in the long term than functional, classical ones. The trouble is that strong colours and sharp contrasts are more difficult to live with. One tires of them more rapidly – and re-decorates more frequently – than one would with gentler, less strongly contrasted schemes.

176 D-I-Y timber and equipment (1)

Does your local authority have a scrap yard? If so, you should be able to buy such items as old floor boards, garden furniture and glass at very reasonable prices. (If you purchase second-hand timber, treat for woodworm by applying one of the branded eradicators.)

177 D-I-Y timber and equipment (2)

Other sources of cheap timber, bricks, tiles, doors, fence pillars and so on are: (a) demolition contractors' yards; (b) nearby houses and shops actually being demolished. For (a), consult the classified section of your telephone directory; for (b), keep your eyes open and, when you spot a demolition site, ask the foreman to let you look around. If you see anything of interest, ask him how much he wants for it.

178 Electrical plug points
It is cheaper to install a double plug point than to put in two, separately. As your need of plug points will probably grow, it is wise to take the long term view and to install them in pairs.

179 Flowers
Make cut flowers last longer by soaking the full length of the stems in cold water for several hours before arranging them. Strip away leaves from the stalks below the water line. Short, cheap flowers can be made to look like long, expensive ones by crumpling up some used kitchen foil and placing it in the vase (not glass, of course) to support the flowers.

180 Furniture
Comfortable and attractive beds, sofas and lounge chairs can be made quite easily and cheaply from plastic foam covered with fabric. Shops which sell the foam usually have instruction leaflets available.

181 Hiring
You can often save money by hiring such equipment as a concrete mixer, floor sander, electric demolition hammer, alloy double extension ladder, spray outfit or gardening equipment for once-in-a-lifetime jobs. Look in the local Yellow Pages for hire companies, phone them to find out if they have the equipment you want, visit two or three and study their catalogues, equipment – and prices.

182 Knife-holder
Screw a number of wooden cotton reels to the inside of a cupboard door, fixing the screws through the centre holes. Fit them as closely together as possible; the gaps between will hold the knife blades without allowing the handles to slip through.

183 Masonry fixing jobs
Before using your electric drill, plug and screw to fit a wooden batten to brick, concrete or breezeblock, consider using masonry pins – they're much cheaper. Apart from the nail, all you need is a hammer.

184   Nest of drawers for screws and nails
Collect 30 or 40 matchboxes, stick them to each other
in three or four stacks of ten, using a contact adhesive or
resin glue. Glue a sheet of thin plywood, cut to exact size,
to the bottom four to form a solid base. Insert a split pin
in the end of each tray to make a little drawer handle.
Slap some paint on the outside of the whole structure
to improve the appearance and to bind it together.

185   Net curtains
The life of net curtains can be prolonged by hemming them
along both top and bottom edges so that they can be
hung either way up. Alternate after each washing.

186   Paint (1)
Paint is expensive – don't waste it. Prevent a skin forming
on the paint in a partially used tin either by storing the
tin upside down or by cutting a disc of tinfoil fractionally
smaller than the tin and floating it on top of the paint.

187   Paint (2)
If you have a tin of paint on which a skin has formed,
stretch an old nylon stocking over the opening of a
new, clean tin, secure the stocking by tying string around
the tin, and pour the old paint into the tin through the
nylon, which acts as a filter.

188   Paint (3)
One way of saving money on the gloss painting of
woodwork is to dilute the paint with a cheaper ingredient;
another is make the paint harder and more permanent
in colour, so that it lasts longer. Both of these things can
be accomplished by adding a little clear varnish *of the
same brand as the gloss paint* to the top coat. Add up to a
quarter pint of gloss varnish to each pint of *white* gloss
paint; add up to three quarters of a pint of gloss varnish
to each pint of *dark* gloss paint.

189   Paint brushes
Soak brushes in cold water for 24 hours before use and
they will last longer. Put them in turps after each usage.
Then shampoo in warm, soapy water. Store by hanging,
bristles downwards, in a cool place. It is worth drilling a
hole through the handle of a paint brush and threading
a length of string through it, so that it may be hung up
after use. This greatly extends its life.

190 Painting

If you are going to prepare and paint new wood with a gloss finish, all the text books tell you to apply wood primer, followed by undercoat, followed by gloss. Undercoat is quite expensive. Many professional decorators substitute this with emulsion paint – it's much cheaper and gives a perfectly satisfactory result.

Obviously, doing your own decorating can save a lot of money. But, to be sure of doing a good job, you may need expert advice. This may be obtained, free of charge from the following:

Berger Paint Advisory Service, Freshwater Road, Dagenham, Essex RM8 IRV (01–599 9924). (Ask for their free booklet *Colour it Berger* and their Brolac and Magicote colour cards.)

Dulux Paints Advisory Service, Imperial Chemical Industries Ltd., Thames House North, Millbank, London SW1P 4QG. (Their leaflet is called *Dulux Complete Painting Guide* and is available from most paint shops as well as from ICI).

Leyland Paint and Wallpaper Advisory Service, Nobel Road, Ely's Estate, Angel Road, Edmonton, London N18 (01–807 8921). The Advisory Service department will give information or advice about interior or exterior decorating.

191 Painting the outside of a house (1)

Fifty to 60% of the cost of having a house painted professionally is swallowed up in labour. On top of this is lumped a profit margin. You can save all this expense by doing the job yourself. But do it thoroughly, scraping off flaking paint, cleaning, sanding, filling and re-priming. Ladders are the problem, of course. Ask around to see if any of your friends could lend you some. If not – and if there are friends or neighbours who would also be prepared to paint their houses if they had ladders – why not get together with them and share the cost of communal ladders?

192 Painting the outside of a house (2)

Amateur house painters often make an expensive mistake. Keen to produce a 'professional finish', they start by removing every scrap of old paint. Depending on the age of the house, they will carefully burn off as many as 20 or 30 layers of perfectly sound paint – and protection –

built up over a period of many years, because they wish to 'get right down to the wood'. This wastes money in two ways: by enormously increasing the amount of primer and undercoat to be used, and by bringing forward the date of the *next* repainting of the house. (It is inevitable that, if you replace a large number of layers of paint with only three or four, the job will not last many years.) An additional hazard is that painting on to raw wood is always slightly risky; if the resin reacts spitefully, the paint may peel completely in a year or two. So, remember that stripping right down to the wood is necessary only when paintwork is truly tatty. Normally, it is best to: remove only the bad spots and areas of flaking paint or bubbles; re-treat those areas with primer and undercoat, if necessary making up to the level of surrounding paint by using a suitable filler; add top coat to everything.

193 Paint smell neutraliser

If you are decorating and cannot bear the smell of paint, don't buy chemical products to mix with the paint — *find some hay*! A handful of hay placed in a bucketful of water will soon remove the odour of paint. Another way is to leave a bowl of salt in the room overnight — but you will have to be prepared for the salt to be ruined.

194 Paintwork

Never wash paintwork with harsh abrasives. A soft cloth dipped in a mild solution of sugar soap will clean and preserve it cheaply and effectively.

195 Picture mounts

Cork tiles (perhaps left over from a job) make impressive, inexpensive picture mounts. Arranged in rectangles along a wall of contrasting colour, they add a different texture to a room, as well as improving its acoustics.

196 Polyfilla substitute

Without doubt, *Polyfilla* is a wonderful product for the D-I-Y man. It comes in various grades for different jobs; it doesn't need wetting in; it stays where you put it; and it is so easy to use that anyone can get a professional finish. But cheap it is not! You can economise on *Polyfilla* by filling most of a large hole — all except the top $\frac{1}{4}$" — with much cheaper *Thistle Plaster* or *Sirapite*, obtainable from any builders' merchant. When it is dry, finish off with *Polyfilla*.

197 Putty or plaster substitute
Instead of using either *Thistle Plaster* or *Sirapite* for filling large holes (see no. 196), you could use home-made substitute plaster, prepared as follows. Boil 3 pints water. Sprinkle $\frac{1}{2}$ lb flour and $\frac{1}{2}$ teaspoon alum into the boiling water. Turn off the heat. Stir. Tear up some old newspapers into small pieces and add to the liquid until a malleable, clay-like consistency is achieved. This makes an efficient filler.

198 Rugs
To make a hard-wearing and attractive rug for no cost whatsoever, you must first save old nylon stockings and tights over a long period. Cut them into strips. Knit, weave or crotchet to the style of your choice.

199 Self-built house
Obviously, enormous sums of money may be saved by building your own house, but you need considerable skill, capital and spare time to attempt such a task. A partial solution to these problems is to erect a timber-framed house — supplied in ready-made sections — on prepared foundations. Write for a list of suppliers to: *Timber Research and Development Association, Central Advisory Service, Hughendon Valley, High Wycombe, Bucks.*

200 Stair carpet
Next time you buy a stair carpet, remember that it's worth purchasing an extra half yard for every flight of stairs. This enables the carpet to be moved a few inches up or down to spread the wear.

201 Tap washers
Did you know that most local Water Boards are perfectly willing to send someone to your house to replace a leaking cold water tap washer, free of charge? You save their water, they'll save your money.

202 Upholstery repairs
Never throw away old sofas or armchairs unless their frames are broken. You can re-upholster them much more easily than you think with the aid of upholstery webbing, $\frac{3}{4}$" tacks and slabs of plastic foam to replace the springs. Nail one end of the webbing to the frame, using three tacks. Pull it as taught as possible to the opposite end of

the frame and secure with three more tacks. Cut off the surplus webbing. Repeat twice more, so that you have three lengths of webbing running parallel with their centres about 5″ apart. Now do the same with pieces of webbing going in the crosswise direction and interweaving with the first three to form a lattice effect. When complete, drop the plastic foam into place to rest upon the webbing base. Re-cover with fabric, using piped seams for extra strength.

203   Vinyl sheeting on quarry tiles
In many ways, sheet plastic is an ideal floor covering for the kitchen. And it's easy to lay and trouble-free – unless your kitchen has a quarry tile floor! You can't put sheet plastic directly on top of quarry tiles without making them sweat unpleasantly. A cheap solution is to lay down sheets of newspaper before positioning the vinyl. This will prevent sweating, *and* save your money!

204   Wallpaper brush
No need to buy a wallpaper brush for smoothing down if you have a large, clean clothes brush which you no longer need.

205   Wallpaper substitute
If you buy a new house, you'll find that it comes with one coat of paint on the plaster. When the time comes to wallpaper, you can fake it. Buy some ceiling whitening and add dye in a pleasing contrast with the present wall colour. Roll up a rag and dip it into your colour. Dab on to the wall to give a stippled effect, with the original wall colour showing through. With care, and by repeating a pattern, you can get an effect very like wallpaper.

206   Windows
Today, there are more ways available of treating a window than ever, and not all of them are expensive. If the view out of the window is attractive, if there is nothing in the room which you wish to conceal from people outside, and if you have double glazing – you do not need to do anything whatsoever to the window. If you have double glazing and also want privacy, a simple canvas roller blind looks good and costs little. Of course, if you do not have double glazing, heavy curtains are an excellent way of keeping in the warmth.

How to save money on
Financial Arrangements

207 Bank account
If you receive a weekly pay packet; if you have your rent collected at the door; if you pay for your gas and electricity by putting coins into a meter; and if you pay cash when shopping, there is little point in having a bank or Giro account. If your bills are few, infrequent and not very large, probably the Giro is the better choice.

208 Bank cards – reward for lost
If ever you find a bank card, take it to the bank and ask about a reward – most banks do give one.

209 Bank charges (1)
Do you inquire about your bank charges and how they are made up? Mistakes are sometimes made. Also, it is possible that you could negotiate an overall reduction if you can agree to make your account more trouble-free for the bank. Ask your bank manager; he will be pleased to help.

210 Bank charges (2)
Ask your bank what is the minimum amount you are allowed to keep in your current account which will make you exempt from charges. Then, make a point of always keeping on the right side, come what may. If your account is permanently above the minimum, open a deposit account on which you will be paid interest. (Bear in mind, though, that the interest is taxable – and also consider saving with a building society.)

211 Bank charges (3)
Did you know that bank charges are decided by the local bank manager and may vary from branch to branch and customer to customer? You should shop around between local banks to see which imposes the lowest charges.

212 Bank charges (4)

You may be surprised to learn that such a fierce battle is being waged between the big four banks that it is possible to persuade them to reduce their 'normal' terms to keep – or to get – your business. Their advertised charges are merely talking points, so don't regard them as final. Banks are as open to haggling as any other business enterprise.

213 Borrowing

Before borrowing money, look at all the various ways in which a loan is available and then work out the real cost of each. There is a simple way of doing this: if you are going to borrow, say, £40 and have to repay eight quarterly sums of £6, you are paying back £48 in all. This means that you are paying £8 in interest (£48–£40), which is 20% of £40. As the period of repayment is two years, divide 20% by 2 to give a crude annual rate of interest of 10%. You now need to make one more calculation to allow for the fact that the outstanding loan is being reduced each quarter. Simply multiply the 10% by 1.8 to give an annual rate of interest of 18%. If repayments are to be made monthly, you should multiply by 1.9; and if weekly, by 2. You now have a fairly accurate assessment of the real credit cost.

214 Borrowing – small loan societies

There are not many mutual self-help societies (small loan companies, friendly societies and non-profit-making credit unions), but they are well worth ferreting out. They lend small amounts to their members for short periods at low rates of interest. Start by looking in the telephone directory's Yellow Pages.

215 Budgeting – annual

If you are trying to survive on a very limited income – perhaps during the first year or so after setting up home – remember that there is only one way to save (or even break even): by not spending one penny more than you need. Obvious? Yes – but do you know how to do it? You must do the same as any big business enterprise – budget! First, you need to plan ahead for 12 months, deciding exactly how your money is to be spent – or saved. The following percentages, the first column of which represents the opinions of several expert home economists, should be helpful.

Item of expenditure	Without a car	With a car
	%	%
Housing (rent, rates, mortgage)	20	20
Household (telephone, laundry, hire purchase repayments, decorating, non-food shopping)	15	12½
Personal (entertainment, meals out, tea/coffee breaks, fares, club subscriptions, hair-dos)	5	2½
Clothes	10	5
Food	30	25
Fuel (oil, gas, electricity, solid fuel)	10	10
Savings and insurance	5	2½
Holidays	5	2½
Car (including petrol, maintenance, garaging, depreciation)	0	20
	100	100

The second column suggests how you may need to adjust your percentages if you are a car owner. Both columns are flexible and you are the only person who can really decide what your priorities should be. The important thing is, having decided them, you should keep to them.

By applying the final percentages to your annual net income, you now convert them into sums of money. For example, if your income after all deductions is £2000, 20% of £2000 for housing is £400; 5% for clothes would be £100, and so on. Next, divide each amount by 12 to give the monthly allocation for that heading (e.g. £400 ÷ 12 = £33.33 for housing). You now need to do a little book-keeping. Get a large-paged exercise book and turn to the first double page spread. Make a column down the left side of the left hand page with all the numbers from 1 to 31 listed, representing the days of the month, with 1 at the top. Rule the rest of the two pages into eight or nine columns (depending upon whether or not you have a car) and write in the headings: 'Housing', 'Household', 'Personal', etc., across the page. Immediately below each heading, write in red ink the monthly allocation for that heading. Now you must keep a strict record, day by day, of every penny spent, entering it in the correct column. At the end of the month, total up your expenditures in each column and compare with the figure in red at the head of the column. This will tell you whether you are under- or over-spent on that heading for the month. Of course, there will be some seasonal items with little expenditure for most of the year, followed by heavy spending for a short period – like fuel bills in the winter or holidays in the summer.

Carry forward the debit or credit for each column to the following month. If there is a sudden, catastrophic increase in the cost of fuel, food, clothing or whatever, you must find ways of cutting down your need for that item – in other words, do without. This book tells you ways of economising on most things.

The advantage of budgeting is that you can see exactly where the money is going; you know immediately if you are spending too much on entertainment or anything else – and you can compensate by spending less upon that item next month. And you really do save money! It may sound like a miserable, penny-pinching existence, but, because you are continually measuring your own progress, you gain a great sense of achievement and a feeling of being in control of the situation.

216 Budgeting – month by month
If you budget as though there were five weeks in every month, you automatically save eight weeks' money per year. But don't forget that, these days, money saved is money devalued. So, do something with it to try to keep pace with loss of value. Invest it, or buy something with it which will rise in value.

217 Credit finding
If you need to find a large and unexpected amount of money, do not raise a second mortgage except as a last resort. It is an expensive way out. If you shop around for a loan between banks and finance houses, you will obtain much more favourable terms. Do not, however, accept the terms on face value. Look into the question of tax relief; it is not always automatically available.

218 Credit cards (1)
If you have the will-power to own a credit card without going on a spending spree, it does give you certain

advantages: you need carry less cash around with you; there is a period of interest-free credit; you don't need to save up before buying something (a good point at a time of rapid price rises); the card company do your bookwork for you; and you pay with only one cheque, which saves bank charges. When you receive your monthly statement from the card company, you may choose to pay off the bill completely or to pay off only a part of it. Should you choose the latter, there will be interest to pay on the outstanding amount – so don't! Pay your credit card company in full and save the interest.

If you are a bit of a spendthrift by nature, however, your best plan is to use your credit card only for scraping mud off your shoes in the winter. The trouble with credit cards is that they have been especially devised to make you and me live beyond our means. I'm strong-minded – but what about you?

219 Credit cards (2)
When you have plenty of cash – as well as credit cards – in your pocket, you could set yourself up in opposition to the credit card companies. Ask the retailer how much discount he pays to the card companies. Then tell him that your terms are half of one per cent less than theirs for cash. It is to his advantage to let you have the item on your terms.

220 Credit cards (3)
Going abroad? Take your credit card with you. Access has international connections through the Interbank Card Association (or Masterchange) and Barclaycard is linked with Ibanco (previously called Bancamericard). This will reduce your purchase of traveller's cheques and foreign currency, both of which are expensive. But take *some* traveller's cheques or currency as a safeguard (see no. 1023). When changing traveller's cheques abroad, be sure to do so at a local bank, *not* in the hotel where you are staying.

221 Credit cards (4)
You *can* use a credit card to draw cash from a bank without using a cheque. Don't do it! The cheque book (or bank card) is cheaper.

222 Credit cards (5)
To get the most out of your credit card, find out from your statement the date on which it is printed out. Then, make

your next big purchases during the last day or two before the next statement is printed. This will mean that the shop-keeper's invoices will not reach the card centre in time to be counted in that month's statement. In this way, you get nearly eight weeks' free credit.

223 House buying, if you are already paying a mortgage
If you are already buying a house, the question is whether or not it is economically sound to stay in it, or to move to a better, more expensive one as a hedge against inflation? Certainly it makes good sense to go into debt at a time of inflation – as long as it is a debt that you will be able to pay off. So, it boils down to job security – how safe is your employment? If there is the slightest danger that you may become redundant, stay in your present home; if you are completely confident that this cannot happen, perhaps you should either move house or, with the aid of a loan from a building society, improve your present home.

224 House buying – first
Let's face it – usually, the trouble with buying your first house is that you wish to do so either at a time when homes are reasonably priced, but no-one will lend you any cash, or when money is available but house prices are ridiculous. The only answer to this is to be, if possible, very patient – and to wait. Every few years there does come a brief, happy period when both houses and money are in plentiful supply.

225 House buying – stamp duty
When you buy a house costing more than £15,000, you have to pay stamp duty, the amount depending on the value of the property. Sometimes, curtains and carpets are included in the price of a house. In this case be sure to deduct a sum representing curtains and carpets *before* the duty is worked out. This is particularly important when the value of the house is just under £15,000 – for the extra cost of curtains and carpets could qualify you to pay £70 or more in stamp duty.

226 House selling – estate agent's fees
There is a tendency to overlook the fees charged by estate agents, or to imagine that all estate agents charge the same fee. This is far from true – fees vary enormously from agent to agent. Therefore, you should shop around the estate agents and ask for their terms to be given in

writing. Narrow it down to three or four reasonable ones and ask all of those to sell your house. When instructing them, say that you have appointed more than one estate agent and intend to pay only the one that makes a sale for you.

227 House improvement (1)
When you own a house, it makes good sense to increase its capital value by improving it. But do not make the common mistake of thinking that all your improvements will add to your house's value. Some will – others won't. Genuine improvements which will certainly increase value are: the addition of a garage (the bigger and more permanent, the better); insulation against cold; central heating; double glazing; a fitted kitchen; and loft conversion. But do not forget that some structural improvements will lead to an increase in rates. And beware of changing fashions! Don't give your house a flat front and picture windows simply because flat fronts and picture windows happen to be in vogue. The fashion will change again, in a few years. And have some respect for the original design, style and outward appearance of your house. Modern looking windows, flush doors and trendy fireplaces may spoil a 60-year-old house rather than improve it. Remember, many 'improvements' are a matter of opinion – they may please you, but horrify a prospective buyer.

228 House improvement (2)
If you are buying a house on a mortgage, it is quite possible that your building society will be prepared to loan you more money for house improvement, either by increasing the amount of your repayments or by extending the repayment period.

229 House improvement (3)
If there is no-one to whom you wish to leave your property, you may have at your disposal a most effective means of raising a large sum of money. You could arrange with an insurance broker to let you have money for house improvement in exchange for the ownership of the house upon your death. If you do not have an insurance broker, contact the *Association of Insurance Brokers, Craven House, 121 Kingsway, London WC2* or the *Corporation of Insurance Brokers, 15 St. Helen's Place, London EC3* for advice on how to proceed.

230   House improvement (4)

Always get permission from your town hall before making any major structural change to your property. Failure to do so could cause the town hall to order you to restore your house to its former state – at your expense, of course – thus causing a double loss.

231   House improvement (5)

Of course, the cheapest way to improve your house, whether by decoration or structural change, is to do it yourself. However, there may be good reasons why you can't do this, so that you are forced to hire a professional. If so, you can save money by shopping around. Never give the job to the first contractor who comes along; first, get four or five quotations. You will find that one firm's price may be as much as double that of another. But be careful ; to give the job automatically to the cheapest firm might be a serious mistake. They _may_ be the cheapest because they are the worst. There's no point in saving a few pounds on decorating a room if the paint peels off within 12 months because the surfaces were not prepared properly. You should be looking for the cheapest firm _which will do a good job_ and your main problem will be recognising them when you find them. The trouble is, a firm may give a very cheap quotation for one of two very different reasons : because they are a cut-price outfit which employs cheap, corner-cutting methods (which prove expensive in the long term) ; or because, although good and reliable, they need some orders quickly.

How can you distinguish between these two types? One way is to insist upon a detailed specification of the job with the quotation. It is only by knowing, for example, how many coats of primer, undercoat and top coat are included for the price that you can make an accurate comparison of quotations. Another good method is to watch for small firms who advertise 'No job too small' – and _give_ them a small job. If they do it well, they will probably also be reliable for larger assignments when these come along.

Don't waste time getting quotations from large firms who do contract work – their prices will only frighten you. And never give work to plausible characters who arrive, uninvited, on your doorstep with theories that your roof needs retiling or your brickwork needs repointing or your front garden needs to be transformed into a parking place. Many of these gentlemen do very inferior work and, later, become very difficult to trace when you wish to tell them so. (See also no. 841.)

232 Income tax – advice
Every March, *Which?* magazine publish Tax-Saving Guides. These give a detailed but clear account of how to complete your income tax returns correctly and to the greatest advantage to yourself. Go to your local reference library and ask to see the guide for the current year.

233 Insurance (1)
When husband and wife both go out to work, it is wise to insure for 'an either way death'. This means that, no matter whether the husband or wife dies first, the house is paid for.

234 Insurance (2)
The price of insurance policies varies greatly from company to company. Therefore, you should never take out long-term insurance without the expert advice of an independent insurance broker who has shopped around on your behalf. How do you find such a broker? Easy! You write to either the *Corporation of Insurance Brokers, 15 St. Helen's Place, London EC3* or the *Association of Insurance Brokers, Craven House, 121 Kingsway, London WC2* and ask for the names of local members.

235 Insurance (3)
Usually, you do not need to insure for the market price of your house because the market price includes the value of the site and this is something which is unlikely to be destroyed. Therefore, you should insure for the cost of rebuilding the house (in the event of it being destroyed) to meet the requirements of local authorities, and including architect's fees and the cost of removing debris, etc.

236 Insurance (4)
Don't let the insurance agent or broker sell you an endowment policy without first finding out whether he can offer 'term insurance', which gives you more cover for less outlay. Endowment policies are splendid – if you can afford them. But term insurance is better for a small premium (although it gives the agent less commission).

237 Life assurance
When taking out your life assurance, be sure to do so in such a way that policies are not classed with your estate for capital transfer tax purposes when you die. Get expert advice on how to avoid this when you buy the assurance. It won't save *you* any money, but it will benefit your next of kin.

238 Money lenders
The average charge made by money lenders is about 40% – but it may be over 50%! So avoid them if at all possible.

239 Money loans – personal
Personal loans from the finance houses are becoming more and more popular. This is hardly surprising as they are available for a wide variety of purposes; they are cheaper than hire purchase finance; and often they are available in larger sums. Usually, the minimum amount available is £100. (When obtaining estimates, look into the question of tax relief; it is not always automatically available.)

240 Mortgage hunting (1)
Generally speaking, there are three classes of mortgage – the ones that are repaid over the loan period, the ones which are not repaid until the end of the loan, and government aid mortgages. As a generalisation, the first group (which includes most council and building society mortgages) is the cheapest. If you pay little or no tax, however, you may be better suited by a government aid mortgage.

241 Mortgage hunting (2)
The more money you borrow, the better for you, so long as house prices continue to rise (and, of course, providing you don't borrow beyond your ability to pay back).

242 Mortgage hunting (3)
If you are a professional employee or civil servant who knows that his salary will rise steadily over the years, you may obtain from some building societies a 'low start mortgage'. This means that you would pay a low rate of interest during the first five years and then increase payments.

243 Mortgage hunting (4)
If you experience difficulty in obtaining a mortgage on a

property which, for some reason, the national building societies will not touch, find out whether there are any small building societies based in that area. You may find that they will be prepared to grant a mortgage — and your problem will be solved.

244 Mortgage hunting (5)
Some insurance companies will make good the difference between the cost of your house and the amount the building society will lend you. But they must first be reasonably convinced that you are fairly well-to-do and a 'good risk'.

245 Mortgage – payment (1)
Thinking of paying off your mortgage? Hesitate at least long enough to work out whether you will be any better off. Remember, you get tax relief on the interest paid on a mortgage.* If your money is in a building society share account, it will be earning you more annual interest than the net interest (after tax relief) which you will save by paying off the mortgage. It is true that, if you retire or are made redundant, your income tax rate may drop to zero. This means that you are a non-tax-payer, so cannot obtain tax relief. Your mortgage, therefore, is costlier than ever! One answer would be to transfer your building society share account funds to some equally safe investment (e.g. British Government stocks, or loans to local councils) which gives a better rate of interest. Another answer is to ask your building society manager whether he can transfer the remains of your mortgage on to an 'option mortgage' basis. This would give you the benefit of a special government subsidy roughly equal to the tax relief which you are no longer getting. But you can only obtain such a transfer on the grounds of hardship.

246 Mortgage – payment (2)
If you are a sitting tenant you may have a chance to buy your home at a favourable rate if the owner wants to realise his assets. Also, if you are a lease-holder, you may be able to buy the freehold under the terms of the Leasehold Reform Act, paying far less than the market price, if bought with vacant possession.

* Tax relief is reduced as a mortgage proceeds; the relief is highest in the early years.

247 Pay packets and pensions

Open your pay packet or draw your pension one day later each week. Every eighth week you will have two, one of which you can save. In one year, you will save six pay packets (or pensions).

248 Pensions – women's

Many women fail to get the best pension rights because they do not think of them as part of their pay. At times, they think there is little point in paying contributions to a pension scheme because the husband will be receiving a pension from his employer. Of course, the husband's pension will be based upon only *his* salary. Therefore, if husband and wife wish to be able to continue the same standard of living when they retire as they have enjoyed on two salaries, they should think in terms of two pensions upon retirement. A wife should try to claim her pension rights, even if she intends to work in a particular firm for only a short term.

249 Rates (1)

First, understand the way the system works ! Rates depend upon two things : the rate poundage as declared annually by the local council (about which you can do nothing), and a valuation of all the property in your area, which is a bit of a generalisation (and which you may be able to get reduced for your house). The two factors are multiplied together to decide how much you should pay. The point is that, when the valuation officers wish to decide the value of the property in your area, they do not inspect each property individually. They merely look at the neighbourhood and ask themselves how much the houses in the area would earn if rented to tenants. They are aware of the main drawbacks in your area – like the new motorway or glue factory – but it is unlikely that they will know about more localised nuisances, like the aroma of curry from an Indian restaurant or the vibration cracks caused by heavy traffic. If you believe you have good cause for a rate reduction, go to your local council or district valuer's office (listed in the telephone directory under 'Inland Revenue') and ask for a form called 'Proposal for Alteration of Valuation List'. Should your application fail to obtain the desired reduction, you may take your case to a Local Valuation Court. If that fails, you can appeal to a Lands Tribunal, but if you lose this one, you may have to pay the costs (so enquire what this could be before commencing proceedings).

250 Rates (2)

Sometimes the residents of a whole street, area or block of flats feel that they have a strong case for rate reduction. There have been several such cases where the desired result has been achieved by everyone banding together to share the costs of professional assistance.

251 Rates (3)

Instead of paying the rates in monthly instalments by banker's order, invest the same amount in a building society share account, where it will earn interest for you. Pay the rates in a lump sum as late as possible or as early as possible, depending on whether or not your local council offers a rebate for early payment.

252 Saving (1)

Inflation may make you wonder whether there is any point in saving. The fact is, there is no point whatsoever in keeping money in a box under the bed because it will only lose value. However, there is every point in making your savings work for you to offset inflation. Generally speaking, there are two ways of doing this: you may earn an income from your savings by loaning your money to some organisation for a period, thus earning interest, or you could make a capital gain by investing your money into something which will increase in value. Whichever method of saving you choose, be sure to check the tax position. Some methods are tax free, whereas others are not.

253 Saving (2)

Indexed-linked saving, recently introduced by the government, is a way of ensuring that your savings do not devalue. There are two schemes. The first is for pensioners, who can save up to £500 and, if they wish, draw it out again one year later, adjusted to allow for changes in the retail prices index.

The other scheme is for anyone who wishes to save up to £20 per month out of his/her earnings, but – unlike the pensioner – he/she must wait five years to gain the full benefit. In both cases, savings are revalued regularly in line with the retail prices index, so that the saver cannot lose by inflation.

254 Saving (3)

Look for ways of saving and borrowing at the same time. This gives you the best of both worlds, as in the case of house buying. You borrow money in the form of a mortgage and also save by getting tax relief on this. It would probably be unwise to pay cash for a house, even if you had it available. There is nothing wrong with borrowing, provided you do not do so beyond your ability to pay back.

255 Saving (4)

There are two golden rules to make saving easier. The first is to enjoy it. You can do this by having an aim – and by looking forward to achieving that aim. Encourage yourself by reading the sales literature about the product for which you are saving. Nothing is more difficult than blind saving without any fixed objective. Second, make saving effortless so that it is easier to save than not. The two best ways of doing this are: to have a standing order which automatically transfers money to a current account at the bank at regular intervals, or to join the Save As You Earn scheme, by which your employer will deduct the savings from your pay packet.

256 Saving schemes

Try a silly saving scheme – they can work in a spectacular way. Years ago, there was a lady in Oldham who never spent half crown pieces. Instead, she threw them on top of a wardrobe. When she eventually got them down, she used them to buy a row of cottages. Today, inflation does not encourage us to hold on to money in this way, because its value is continually falling. So, if you decide not to spend any more 2p pieces, you should pay them regularly into a savings account where they will gain interest.

257 Subscriptions

Before buying an annual subscription to anything, (a) ask yourself whether this is an interest that will continue over the years. If you believe it is, (b) find out whether it is possible to buy a life subscription. These cost more but are extremely economical in the long term, especially if you are quite young at the time of taking them out. Furthermore, subscriptions – like everything else – tend to become more and more expensive, so there is a secondary saving in buying at today's prices. Example:

annual membership of the National Trust costs £3 and entitles only one person to visit NT properties free. A further £1.50 must be paid for a second member of the family. But a life membership, costing £50, enables two family members to visit properties, free of charge, for the life of the member. This is already a bargain but will become more so if and when the subscription goes up.

258 Valuations for insurance
When you buy jewellery, furs or anything else of value which you may want to have insured, be sure to get a written valuation before you leave the shop. If you don't, you will need to pay a fee for a valuation at the time of insuring. Also, the value put upon the article by the seller may be a little higher than a value given by an independent valuer.

How to save money on
Food

259 Apple and potato peelings
If you throw away the peelings from an apple or potato, you throw away its most nutritious part. Instead, make sure the peelings are clean. Mince. Use.

260 Apple rings – evaporated
They may look expensive, but did you realise that 1 lb of evaporated apple rings soaked in water for 24 hours gives the equivalent of 5 lb of fresh fruit?

261 Apples
The best way to store apples for the winter is to pack them in layers in a bin (not touching one another), alternating with layers of dry sand. The sand keeps out air and moisture.

262 Apple wine
A home-made wine enthusiast? Try apple peelings. $\frac{3}{4}$ lb of peelings are needed to produce three pints of wine.

263 Asparagus substitute
Inexpensive spinach is rich in vitamin C and has far more food value than asparagus.

264 Avocado substitute
Try an ordinary dessert pear instead of an avocado, with the core scooped out and sprinkled with lemon juice. Fill in the usual way.

265 Bacon (1)
Middle-cut slices are more economical than prime back. Fresh-cut bacon is better value than vacuum pre-packed.

266 Bacon (2)
Shop at a grocer's where they will slice your bacon as thinly as possible. In this way, 1 lb of bacon can seem more like 2!

267 Bacon (3)
Don't underrate bacon pieces – for many dishes they are

just as good as bacon. If too fatty, the surplus fat may be rendered down by slow heating in a pan.

268 Baking powder
Make your own baking powder with two teaspoons of cream of tartar and one teaspoon of bicarbonate of soda. This would make enough to use with 1 lb of plain flour.

269 Bananas
There are two kinds of banana eaters: those who like the fruit over-ripe and those who don't. If you belong to the second category, do not throw away bananas simply because they have turned mushy. Instead, fry them in butter and brown sugar with just a spot of lemon juice. (If you do like soft bananas, have you tried them as a sandwich spread?)

270 Batter for coating
Instead of expensive eggs, use flour and water. Alternatively, make a custard powder and water batter.

271 Beef
When comparing joints of meat for value, note the proportion of meat to bone. If half-and-half, double the stated price. If one-third bone, add a half to the price. When you do this, you will sometimes find that 'expensive' cuts of lean meat are the cheapest after all. Best value is lean brisket, rolled and boned.

272 Biscuits (1)
If you like cheese and biscuits but resent the high cost of the biscuits, here is a recipe for Norwegian flatbread which will solve your problem: Mix 8 oz wholewheat flour, 4 oz soya flour and a little salt with cold water to make a stiff dough. Roll out very thin. Prick with fork. Cut into rounds. Bake for about 6 minutes in a hot (450° or mark 8) oven until crisp.

273 Biscuits (2)
Never keep biscuits and cake in the same tin – unless you like limp biscuits.

274 Biscuits (3)
Some shops sell loose, broken biscuits very much more cheaply than packeted biscuits. You can't eat biscuits without breaking them – so why not buy them pre-broken?

275 Blackberry wine
Collect a 1-gallon bucketful of blackberries and place fruit in a large container. Boil 1 gallon of water and pour over the berries. Add 1 campden tablet. Cover container and let stand for one week, stirring daily. Do not mush the blackberries. Prepare a syrup from a little of the juice heated and mixed with 3 lb of sugar. When cool, strain rest of juice into it, stir and add the juice of 1 lemon. Put into a fermentation jar. Add ¾ oz yeast. Allow to ferment. Draw off from the lees. Mature. Bottle.

276 Boiled ham
If you don't do anything to prevent it, boiled ham will go dry, leathery and discoloured, like last summer's sandals. Always wrap it in wet, greaseproof paper.

277 Boiling bacon
For a medium sized family (four or five people) best bacon value is a whole fore-hock, boned and rolled. The meat will go further if carved from both ends. For a smaller family (two or three people), 2 lb of bacon from the lean end of the fore-hock gives a joint that is leaner and firmer textured than collar, although usually costing the same.

278 Bread (1)
Bought bread costs about three times as much as home-baked bread, which you can make as follows: Ingredients: 3 lb plain flour; 2 oz lard; ¾ oz dried yeast; 1½ pints tepid water; 3 teaspoons salt. Sieve the flour and salt into a bowl. Measure ½ pint of water into a jug and sprinkle the yeast on to it. Leave for about 10 minutes until frothy. Cut lard into small pieces, rub into flour. Add yeast mixture and a little water. Knead until dough is smooth and springy. Place in bowl dusted with flour and leave until it doubles in size. Knead again and break into 5 pieces. Leave until double in size. Brush with egg or milk. Bake at 425° or mark 7 for 20 minutes.

279 Bread (2)
Given a steady hand and a sharp bread knife, a large, unsliced loaf is better value for money than either two small loaves or one large sliced loaf. Not only is it cheaper, it keeps better (if put in a plastic bag).

280 Bread (3)
Dip the bread knife into hot water occasionally when

cutting bread, drying before use each time. It will be found to cut more thinly.

281 Bread (4)

Stale loaves should never be thrown away. Brush them over with milk and bake in a moderate oven for 15 minutes. This freshens the bread and gives it a new lease of life. An alternative method is to dip quickly into cold water and then bake.

282 Bread (5)

Whether you buy bread or (better) bake your own (see no. 278) never waste any. If you do buy, get the large, unsliced loaf. Whatever odd bits of bread you do not need immediately, wrap in foil and keep in the fridge. Even small pieces will be useful for making breadcrumbs.

283 Bread – left over:
Bread and butter pudding – savoury (serves four)

Cut crusts off 6 slices white bread. Spread with butter or margarine. Cut into squares or fingers. Put 3 slices into a greased 2-pint casserole dish. Sprinkle with 3 oz grated Cheddar cheese. Top with rest of bread. Beat 3 eggs with 1 pint milk. Season with salt, pepper and mustard to taste. Pour gently over bread and cheese. Leave to stand for ½ hour. Sprinkle remaining cheese on top. Bake in centre of moderate oven (325° or mark 3) for ¾ to 1 hour or until golden brown and firm.

284 Bread – left over:
Bread and butter pudding – sweet

This is still one of the cheapest and easiest of desserts to make. Take some left-over slices of bread and butter (or some stale bread, and butter or margarine them). Put 2 slices in the bottom of a well greased casserole dish. Sprinkle sultanas or raisins, sliced to give full flavour, or chopped dates. Add another layer of bread, followed by more fruit, and so on until the dish is half full. Whisk up 2 eggs and stir in a dessertspoon of sugar until dissolved, add 1 pint of milk and pour mixture slowly over bread. Leave for 1 hour until saturated. Cook in fairly cool oven for about 1 hour.

285 Bread – left over: breadcrumbs

Make left over bread into fine breadcrumbs by sieving, and drying in the oven. Store in air-tight jars.

286 Bread – left over: Queen of Puddings

As a change from sweet bread pudding, try Queen of Puddings. Put 2 oz of breadcrumbs in a basin with 2 egg yolks and 1 oz sugar. Beat well and add $\frac{3}{4}$ pint warm milk. Spread 2 tablespoons jam or fruit *purée* over base of 2-pint pie dish and put the breadcrumb mixture on top. Cook for about 45 minutes in centre of moderate oven (325° or mark 3). Whisk the 2 egg whites stiffly. Add 3 oz sugar, carefully folding it in with a metal spoon. Spread pudding with 2 oz of jam or *purée*, then top with meringue. Return to oven for further 20 to 25 minutes. Serve hot.

287 Bread – left over: toast

Left over bread, if thick enough, may be made into very fine toast by cutting into wafer-thin slices and crisping in a moderate oven.

288 Bread soup (serves four or five)

Heat 1 oz margarine in pan. Add 2 medium onions, chopped, and 1 chopped clove garlic. Cover pan and fry gently until contents are soft but not browned. This will take about 10 minutes. Add $1\frac{1}{2}$ pints chicken stock made from cubes and 3 large slices of white bread. Bring to boil, whisking continually. Heat $\frac{1}{4}$ pint milk and 1 egg together. Take soup from heat. Add egg mixture. Mix well. Season with salt and pepper to taste. Transfer to warm soup bowls. Sprinkle with parsley. (Vegetarians could use water from vegetables like cabbage, carrots, peas or beans, instead of chicken stock.)

289 Bread – stale

Don't throw it away! Cut into fingers, coat thinly with beaten egg and fry with bacon for breakfast. Alternatively, fry in butter and serve with jam for tea.

290 Butter (1)

Blended butter is the best value for money, but unblended butter keeps better in warm weather.

291 Butter (2)

Don't try to scrape your butter dish clean with an ordinary knife – it's impossible. Instead, use a spatula. This bends to the task and produces far more butter.

292 Butter (3)

Beat $\frac{1}{2}$ lb butter until soft. Mix in 2 fl. oz of hot water. The butter will now spread more thinly, as well as being greater in bulk – a double economy.

293   Butter (4)
Mix ½ lb of your usual butter with ¼ lb cheapest margarine and add the cream from the top of the milk and a pinch of salt. Mix thoroughly. The end product will taste remarkably like undiluted butter.

294   Cabbage and cauliflower leaves
Do you throw away the dark green, rather tough outer leaves of a cabbage or cauliflower? If so, you are throwing away the most nourishing part of the vegetable. You should chop them into small pieces and cook.

295   Cake
Best value are: slab cake sold by weight; the plain round sponge cakes to which you add your own filling.

296   Cake – left over
Make into fritters by cutting into slices, dipping in beaten egg and frying in hot butter until golden. Serve, topped with jam. (And, of course, there's always trifle. But remember that the secret of a good trifle is not to have too much sweetness. A touch of dryness – perhaps from a dry sherry – makes all the difference.)

297   Cake – sponge
Before buying a packet of sponge sandwich mix, re-member that you will need to add the cost of eggs, jam (or other filling), butter and cooking fuel. Ready-made jam sponges work out at about half the cost, as well as saving time.

298   Canned foods
Many supermarkets have a special display of battered and dented cans of fruit or vegetables which are sold very cheaply. Provided the air has not got into the cans, the only thing wrong with them is their appearance. Inspect carefully for signs of rust or leaking before buying. Never buy canned goods which bulge outwards because these probably do contain air.

299   Canned luncheon meat
The Danish brands usually give best value for money. A 12-oz can of corned beef is more economical than slices.

300 Casserole (1)
Casserole cooking is cheap cooking, especially when you use the cheaper cuts of meat.

301 Casserole (2)
Freezer owners can save by cooking three casseroles at the same time. Eat one on the same day; freeze the others. No freezer? Then cook two; cool one quickly and put in the fridge for the next day. Re-heat it rapidly in a pan on top of the cooker.

302 Casserole – left over beef
Dice the beef small. Add to a can of heated vegetable soup. Stir in a little mustard for extra flavour.

303 Casserole – left over chicken
Dice the left over chicken and add to a mushroom or asparagus soup. Add corn or mixed vegetables or green or red peppers (tinned or fresh).

304 Casserole – left over duck, lamb or pork
The thinner soups are better with duck. So dice into a canned *consommé* and heat. Thicken with cornflour just before serving. Left over lamb and pork can be heated in a *consommé* in the same way.

305 Casserole – left over ham
Dice the ham and put into a tomato or cream of chicken soup. Add mushrooms, corn or grated carrot for extra flavour.

306 Castor sugar
Expensive castor sugar can be made from less expensive granulated sugar by using the blender or coffee grinder. (Keep the machine running a little longer and you have icing sugar.)

307 Cat food
If you own a kitten, don't spoil it. Be sure to bring it up to have wide and sophisticated tastes in its personal eating habits. A choosey cat can cost you a small fortune in cat foods. But, in the right hands, and if started young enough, a cat may acquire a taste for beans, bacon rind, sprouts, stale cheese, scraps of old bread and butter and cold tea, as well as meat pieces of every kind.

308 Celery salt substitute
Instead of expensive celery salt, for the flavouring of soups

use washed and dried celery leaves, finely chopped.

309 Cheese (1)
Did you know that most supermarkets and grocers keep a box of 'cheese ends', 'cheese bits' or 'stale cheese' which they sell off cheaply? Ask! The cheese is sometimes not distinguishable from the much dearer 'ordinary' kind and is ideal for cooking.

310 Cheese (2)
If you slice your cheese with a potato peeler, you will find the cheese lasting longer and the sandwiches tasting better.

311 Cheese (3)
When cheese goes rock-like and seemingly inedible, do not throw it away. Instead, grate it and store in a jar ready for all those soups and pasta dishes where the recipe says: 'Sprinkle well with Parmesan'. It would take a good gourmet to tell the difference. (Also see no. 440 – Sandwich Spread.)

Alternatively, if you wish to soften the cheese, try soaking it in buttermilk.

312 Cheese (4)
Best method of storing cheese is not in the fridge. Wrap the cheese in greaseproof paper and put under inverted plant pot which has previously been well soaked in cold water.

313 Cheese (5)
Cheese that has been grated goes further in cooking and in sandwiches. So grate all your grateable cheese and store in screw-top jars.

314 Cheese (6)
Freshly cut cheese is much better value for money than pre-packed.

315 Cheaper meals
Have you considered going vegetarian? Health, moral and religious arguments aside, there is certainly a strong economic case in favour of vegetarianism. For a start, milk, cheese and bread are comparatively cheap. Then, vegetable protein is cheaper than meats and takes less time (and fuel) to cook. Today, one can buy dehydrated protein foods, which are claimed to be more

nutritious than meat for only a fraction of the cost. Write for further information to: _The Vegetarian Centre, 53 Marloes Road, London W8 6LD._

316 Cheap, tasty protein
Have you ever tasted pigs' fry, pigs' trotters, brains, sweet-breads, cowheel, ox cheek or tripe? If not, ask yourself why. Could it be that you have been put off by the idea? A little squeamish, perhaps? If that is so, consider these points. First, all of these foods can be made into tasty and nutritious meals. Second, by the time those meals are prepared, the ingredients do not resemble the originals any more than fried bacon resembles sliced pig; on your plate, they are simply appetizing foods. Third, they are all cheap. (By using them, you can take advantage of other people's squeamishness!)

317 Chicken or turkey (1)
You can make a cheap old boiling fowl tender by rubbing it with lemon juice, wrapping in a sheet of greaseproof paper and steaming for a minimum of three hours.

318 Chicken or turkey (2)
Best value for money are the oven-ready birds, especially the larger ones. When comparing prices of fresh and frozen birds, remember that about 11% of the weight of the latter is frozen water. To allow for this, subtract one-tenth from the stated weight and divide its price by the answer to give the cost per oz. For a fresh bird, simply divide the price by the number of oz.

319 Chutney
You can use up vegetable stalks and apple cores by making chutney.

320 Chutneys/salad dressing
When the last pickled onion has been taken from the bottle, one is usually left with about 2″ of rather murky vinegar. Save it for chutneys and (after straining) for salads.

321 Clover wine
Pick 1 gallon of clover flowers. Place in large container. Pour 1 gallon boiling water over the flowers and allow to cool till lukewarm. Then add 3 lb white sugar, 3 lemons, 2 oranges, 1 oz yeast. Stir and leave to stand for 4 days before straining and bottling.

322 Cocoa
In terms of nourishment per penny, cocoa is better value for money than either tea or coffee – but you may find it difficult to change if you're hooked on one of the latter.

323 Cocktail sausages
If your cocktail parties go better with lots of little sausages impaled upon sticks, but you object to paying more per lb for them, here's good news. You can solve your problem if you buy the required weight of chipolata sausages and perform a small manipulative operation on each. Squeeze the sausage around its waist so that the meat is pushed away from the middle, leaving a small pocket of nothing. Twist the two halves of the sausage, creating two mini-sausages. Cut the joining skin.

324 Coffee – genuine
Best value for money is either a blend of Kenya and Mocha or of Brazilian and Costa Rican. They both provide drinkable coffee at reasonable cost.

325 Coffee substitute
Dandelion roots, if dried and ground, make a very good coffee substitute. Unlike real coffee, it can be taken as a sleep-inducing bed-time drink.

326 Cooking fat (1)
Use an old margarine or butter wrapper to rub down the frying pan before a fry-up.

327 Cooking fat (2)
Bacon fat is delicious and it is a pity to waste any of it. After frying bacon for breakfast, do not clean out the frying pan but simply place a lid upon it in readiness for any other frying, later in the day. Or, if you are left with a large quantity of bacon fat, pour it into a container and keep it for the frying of anything except fish.

328 Cooking fat (3)
Sausages produce a lot of fat when fried. Let it cool, then pour into a container and keep in the fridge for future use. But do not mix with bacon fat.

329 Cream
To make fresh or canned cream go further, stir in the cream from the top of the milk.

330 Cream alternative
Evaporated milk is very cheap and very rich in vitamin D.

331 Cream – double
Here's how to get single cream to whip like double cream: First, whip the white of an egg. Then, whip the single cream thoroughly. Combine the two.

332 Cream filling
Canned cream does not normally thicken on beating, so it's not usually used as a filling. Canned cream does go firm when chilled, though. So, put a can into the fridge and leave for 12 hours. Open can and carefully pour away the liquid. Add small amount vanilla essence to cream, stirring in gently with a fork.

333 Cream – home-made
Make your own cream. Boil $\frac{1}{4}$ pint from the top of the milk. Add $1\frac{1}{2}$ oz unsalted butter. Beat thoroughly. Cool in the fridge. When cold, beat vigorously again.

334 Cream – whipping (1)
This is much cheaper than double cream and whips well to a softish consistency. However, it is not easily obtainable in all areas. Make home-made whipping cream by combining equal quantities of single and double cream and whipping until stiff.

335 Cream – whipping (2)
You can buy a little rubber and plastic gadget for syphoning the cream off the top of a bottle of milk. If you do this with 'gold top' milk, the cream will whip. You can often substitute the top of the milk (unwhipped) for single cream in recipes.

336 Dates
Dried-up dates may be revived by placing them in a pudding cloth (or piece of soft net) in the top of a double boiler for five minutes.

337 Dog food
Lights are a good, cheap food for the dog – if used properly. The golden rule is: do not feed them to your dog undiluted, as a complete replacement for his usual meat. Instead, substitute lights for about one third of his normal meat – and watch him for a few days to make sure that the new diet agrees with him.

338 Dripping
Don't forget that you can re-use fat repeatedly for deep-frying if you continually clarify it by straining.

339 Egging and crumbling
Some dishes look really tasty finished off with a coating of egg and breadcrumbs. But eggs are expensive. In future, save the egg by mixing a little custard powder with water to make a thin cream. Also, to use egg to colour pastry is 'eggstravagant'. Custard powder and water will do for that, too.

340 Eggs (1)
Brown eggs cost more than white ones partly because many people prefer them, and also – according to the British Egg Information Service – because the brown hens who lay them are a heavier breed, needing more food. But there is no difference whatsoever in nutritional value.

341 Eggs (2)
When a recipe calls for only the yolk or the white of an egg, what do you do with the other part? Left over whites may be: added to scrambled eggs or omelettes; made into meringues; stored in a covered container; or used to make single cream whip like double (see no. 331). Left over yolks may be added to soups or sauces or placed in a cup, covered with water, and stored in the fridge.

342 Egg substitute (1)
When your cake recipes tell you to use 2 eggs, use only 1 but add a dessertspoon of vinegar. Result: the cake tastes just as good – and it's lighter.

343 Egg substitute (2)
When coating food with egg and it seems that you're not going to have enough, do not use another egg. Mix the existing egg with a little milk – it will go further.

344 Egg substitute (3)
For puddings requiring 2 eggs, substitute 1 dessertspoon of cornflour for 1 of the eggs. For scrambled egg or omelettes, decrease the number of eggs used and add 1 tablespoon of milk for each egg included. This will make up the bulk.

345 Egg white substitute
A useful egg white substitute may be made by mixing 1

teaspoon of powdered gelatine with 2 tablespoons of hot – but not boiling – water. Leave to cool before use.

346 Elderberries
Most people know that elderberries make excellent wine, but not many use them to eke out the apples in the making of pies. Perhaps the reason is that they don't know the easy way of removing the small berries from the elder twigs – by combing them off with a kitchen fork.

347 Elderberry soup
Collect 1 lb elderberries (strip fruit from stalks by combing with a fork and wash well). Put in pan with $1\frac{3}{4}$ pints water. Add a little lemon rind and simmer until tender. Either put berries through a blender or rub them through a fine sieve. Put back in pan and bring to boil once again. Mix $\frac{3}{4}$ oz cornflour with a little water. Add this to *purée*, stirring continuously until completely cooked. Season with lemon juice and $3\frac{1}{2}$ oz sugar. Serve hot or cold with *croûtons* of fried bread.

348 Elder flower fritters
Fancy an elder flower fritter? Pick the elder flowers when they are just opening. Wash, dip in thin batter, fry and sprinkle with sugar.

349 Fasting for fitness
Yoga not only makes you feel fit – it decreases your appetite, thus saving food.

350 Fish
Fish is still one of our cheapest and most nourishing foods. Watch prices and buy when cheap – for example, late on Saturday afternoon (if you have a market). Watch out for 'unfashionable' fish. Many of these taste just as good and provide as much nourishment as our traditional cod, haddock, herring, etc. So why haven't we eaten them before? Very often, the answer is: because they are so *ugly* that people are put off by their appearance. So, next time you see a particularly repulsive (but cheap) catfish on the fishmonger's slab, remind yourself that it tastes like halibut.

351 Fish – canned
Best value are herrings, mackerel, pilchards and tuna. Pink salmon is cheaper than sockeye simply because it does not *look* as salmony – but it has exactly the same

food value. Incidentally, salmon is more nutritious and cheaper than best steak.

352 Fish fingers
Best value are the ones you make for yourself by dipping fish into home-made batter. If you must buy ready-made ones, large fish fingers are better value than small ones (too much of which is breadcrumbs).

353 Fish hot-pot (serves four)
Slice 1 lb part-boiled potatoes fairly thinly. Remove any skin or bones from a coley fillet which has been cooked, and flake the fish. Fry 2 sliced, medium sized onions gently in 1 oz margarine until pale gold. In another pan, melt $1\frac{1}{2}$ oz margarine in $1\frac{1}{2}$ oz flour for 2 minutes without browning. Gradually, blend in $\frac{1}{2}$ pint milk and $\frac{1}{2}$ pint stock (fish, vegetable or chicken). Cook while stirring until sauce comes to boil and thickens. Continue to cook for 2 minutes. Season with salt and pepper. Add 1 or 2 teaspoons continental mustard. Fill a fairly deep, greased casserole dish with alternate layers of (a) potatoes, fish and fried onions, and (b) sauce, beginning and ending with the potatoes. Cover with cheese. Reheat and brown towards top of moderately hot oven (400° or mark 6) for 20–30 minutes.

354 Fish – left over
Fish spoils more rapidly and easily than any other food, so left over fish should be used as soon as possible. There are three classic ways of doing this : (a) Serve cold with a salad. (b) Fish cakes. (Mix fish with equal amounts of mashed or dehydrated potatoes. Bind with an egg. Form into round cakes. Dip in seasoned flour and coat with beaten egg and crisp breadcrumbs. Fry in hot fat until crisp and brown.) (c) Fish pie. (Flake fish. Blend with chopped, hard-boiled eggs and anchovy or a white cheese or parsley sauce. Put in pie dish. Top with potato and small pieces of butter. Cook in centre of moderately hot oven for about 30 minutes until heated through and crisp and brown on top.)

355 Fish sauce
If your family are not madly enthusiastic about such white fish as 'rock' or coley, you can make these fish more interesting by adding a tasty sauce. One of the cheapest – and easiest – ways of producing such a sauce is to use one

of the condensed soups in its condensed form. Mushroom, tomato and celery are all suitable. One pound of coley baked with a tin of condensed mushroom soup, plus a vegetable, makes a very acceptable meal for four people.

356 Flavourings for puddings
Never throw away orange peel. Dry it. Grate. Use for flavouring sweets.

357 Flour (1)
Food mixers have a nasty, wasteful habit of spitting flour all over the kitchen floor or walls. Discourage this by covering your mixer with a tea-towel.

358 Flour (2)
Instead of throwing away that empty flour bag, coat your next piece of meat or fish by placing it inside the bag and shaking about.

359 Freezer – filling the
When you buy your freezer and you learn that it needs to be at least three-quarters full to run economically, you may wonder how on earth to fill it quickly. Three suggestions: large quantities of bread, large packs of vegetables, or, if these are too expensive, ice bags.

360 Freezers (1)
Freezers enable you to take advantage of low seasonal prices of fruit and vegetables. There are hundreds of bulk suppliers of frozen food in Britain, most of whom will deliver to your home if given an order worth at least £5. With experience, you should be able to save about 25% on food bills by buying in bulk.

361 Freezers (2)
Freezers are also great for reasons of convenience – you always have food in the house and it is more varied than would otherwise be possible. But be careful if your main interest is economy! It is true that a freezer *can* be a real saving if you grow your own vegetables, can buy cheap bulk offers, or can get supplies of really cheap meat. For it to pay its way, however, you need to save about 4p per lb when it's fully packed.

The UK Association of Frozen Food Producers gives useful information about the handling of frozen foods. They also deal with complaints that have first been made without satisfaction to the retailers and manufacturers. *The UK AFFP, 1/2 Castle Lane, Buckingham Gate, London SW1E 6DL.*

Information about deep freezing and freezers may be obtained from: *The Food Freezer Committee, 25 North Row, London W1R 1DJ.*

362 Freezing eggs
Freezing eggs can be a problem, yet it is well worth doing because of the way prices fluctuate. Open-freeze the beaten eggs (with added salt or sugar, as required) in plastic margarine tub lids – one egg per lid. When solid, remove from lid and pack like beefburgers, interleaving with plastic. If you don't have enough plastic lids, open-freeze the eggs in those little waxed paper cases used for making small cakes.

363 Freezing fish fillets
Instead of struggling to skin fish fillets before freezing, and thus wasting some of the fish, freeze them with the skin on. Then when fillets are needed for use, take them out of the freezer and place in cold water for four or five seconds. You will find that the skin rips off, leaving the fillet whole and still frozen.

364 Fresh lemons
Whole lemons are best kept in cold water.

365 Fresh fish
Best all-round, protein for pence value is mackerel.

366 Fruit
Fruit goes further in a crumble (or crumbly crust) pie than in an ordinary fruit pie. Also, you can get away with cheap quality fruit if mixed with the more expensive.

367 Fruit and tomatoes
Don't buy the pre-packed variety – you're paying extra for the spick and span appearance. Once you take the apple out of the plastic, it's just another apple, like the ones you buy loose.

368 Fruit and vegetables
These keep better if you don't wash them till just before use.

369 Fruit cake (1)
Perhaps you like rich fruit cake, but, not being rich

yourself, find it rather expensive to make. Never mind!
You can turn a not-very-fruity fruit cake into a juicy
success by chopping the raisins and sultanas before
mixing them in.

370 Fruit cake (2)
Dried elderberries and chopped prunes make a fruit
cake every bit as fruity flavoured as the more usual –
more expensive – currants and raisins.

371 Fruit – canned
The prices of canned fruit vary enormously according
to crop sizes. However, the bargains to look for are no. 2
size English rhubarb and South African sliced peaches
and pineapple in heavy syrup. Check to see how the
canned prunes compare with the dried prunes – sometimes they are cheaper.

372 Fruit – left over
Three ways of using up cooked fruit are: (a) Add to
jellies (taking care to measure the juice so that you do not
exceed the correct amount of liquid). (b) Make into a
smooth *purée* and use to make a 'fruit fool' by blending
with equal amount of whipped cream or thick custard
and putting into glasses, chilling and topping with
cream. (c) Make into a *purée*; beat in the yolks of 2
eggs; cook for $\frac{1}{2}$ hour in a moderate oven; top with
meringue mixture made from egg whites and sugar;
return to oven for further 25 minutes – and you have a
'fruit amber'. Serve hot.

373 Gammon
Gammon will shrink dramatically when boiled or baked
unless you foil it – by wrapping in aluminium foil.

374 Ground almond substitute
Add a few drops of almond essence to fine semolina
and you have a substitute for ground almonds that will
fool anyone by the time it is baked into a cake or pastry.

375 Hamburgers
Home-made hamburgers are made more succulent by
the inclusion of a grated raw potato (which also makes
them bigger).

376 Herbs
If you use herbs in your cooking, why not grow your

own? Sage, mint, thyme, parsley, rosemary and chives can all be home grown fairly easily in a window box or plant pot. You pick the leaves and hang them to dry, preferably out of doors where the rain can't reach them (an open shed is ideal). When the leaves are completely dry and shrivelled, strip them from stems and rub through a fine sieve or crush with a rolling pin. Store in dark bottles with tight stoppers, never in paper or cardboard cartons.

377 Ice cream
Are you aware that you can now buy one-gallon and half-gallon plastic tubs of ice cream at very economical prices? If you don't have a freezer it can be kept perfectly well in the ice-making compartment of the ordinary fridge. Cut-price freezer food centres, stocking well-known brands of all sorts of commodities, are now to be found in many areas.

378 Jam
The 1-lb jars of good quality jam from Bulgaria, Hungary and Poland are excellent value at low cost. Compare prices and weights of other jams – some jars which appear to hold 1 lb actually contain only 12 oz.

379 Jam-making (1)
All the recipes tell you to use preserving sugar. Granulated is much cheaper and the results are perfectly satisfactory.

380 Jam-making (2)
Do not skim jam as it boils. This is wasteful and is better done after jam has reached setting point and finished cooking. A knob of butter or margarine stirred in at the end helps to disperse any skin that remains.

381 Jam-making (3)
Rhubarb is an excellent 'jam filler'. It goes well with other fruits, adding little flavour of its own and, therefore, not clashing. It is comparatively cheap and enables a more expensive fruit to go further.

382 Jelly
Both crab apples and sloes make good, inexpensive jelly.

383 Knuckle of bacon
Knuckle of bacon is hard to beat as a bargain buy. For only a few pence per pound it gives: meat enough for a main meal for two (after gentle simmering with bay leaf

and herbs) ; two or three tasty sandwiches ; scraps for use in omelettes ; the stock for lentil soup ; a bone for the dog ; and rind for the birds (or for soup stock – see no. 454).

384 Lemons
Before squeezing a lemon, heat it in the oven (but only if you are already using the oven for something else). This way the lemon will give much more juice.

385 Lemon squash
Squeeze 6 lemons into a jug. Cut up all the peel and add. Pour in 3 pints cold water, 3 lb sugar and 2 oz citric acid. Leave for 4 or 5 hours, giving an occasional stir. Strain off the solids and bottle the concentrated lemon squash. Dilute to taste when using.

386 Main course economy
You can save a sizeable amount of a main course by serving soup as a first course (with filling bread rolls, of course!).

387 Margarine
When a recipe instructs: 'use soft margarine', don't! Use the hard margarine – it may take longer to cream, but it's also a lot cheaper.

388 Marmalade (1)
The 2-lb tins of South African or Australian marmalade are the best buys.

389 Marmalade (2)
By all means make your own marmalade – but don't waste time and money using your own ingredients. Instead, try a tin of the concentrated marmalade mix. It's good and it's cheap.

390 Marmalade – chunky
If you like 'butch' marmalade, buy the marmalade concentrate available in tins (see no. 389) and prepare according to the instructions. But before you begin cooking it, take the peel from two fresh oranges, wash and chop into small pieces and strips. Put in water and cook until tender. Sieve. Now begin heating the concentrate. Add the peel during boiling.

391 Marzipan
To make a reasonable mock marzipan (sufficient to cover an 8"-diameter cake), cream 2 oz butter, 2 oz castor sugar

and 2 teaspoons of almond essence. Blend in $\frac{1}{2}$ lb Madeira cake crumbs. Knead well until it resembles real almond paste.

392   Meal for four

A cheap meal for four people: Cut the top off a 1-lb loaf and scoop out most of the inside (keeping the bread-crumbs for the top of your next casserole). Leave a 'loaf shell' with 1"-thick walls. Fill this case with a savoury mixture of minced meat, vegetables and sauce. Put back the top crust, like a lid, and roast in a moderate oven until hot all the way through. Slice and serve. It will taste delicious and it will not be necessary for you to add any garnishings (as you would with a pie).

393   Meal for two

Packet soup is all very well, but it's hardly a meal, is it? To turn it into a meal, make several small (prune-size) dumplings and cook with the soup. Simmer for 15 minutes with a lid on the pan.

394   Meal from left overs

Don't forget the humble rissole as a way of using up every scrap. Mix left over fish or meat with breadcrumbs. Add a beaten egg, salt and pepper. Shape into rissoles and fry until golden brown.

395   Meals (1)

Experiment with wines, herbs and spices and use them to add interest to cheap meals.

396   Meals (2)

Try inexpensive health-giving additives – like wheat germ – to increase the value of cheap, tasty dishes. Wheat germ can be used with soup, stewed fruit, minced meat or flour in baking.

397   Meat (1)

Because meat is now so expensive, there's all the more need for careful buying. Rib, brisket or casserole steak are all good buys. Three people can have a good meal for under 50p from a casserole. Instead of leg of pork, try shoulder and spare rib (boned and rolled) or stuffed belly. A boned and rolled shoulder blade end of lamb is just as sweet as leg of lamb. Chump ends cost about one third as much as lamb chops and are just as good casseroled. Neck of mutton makes a delicious stew.

398 Meat (2)

If you do not own a mincer, get one. It will put money in your bank. With a mincer, you can make the toughest, cheapest cut of meat from the butcher's into an easily cooked mince which is just as nourishing as any of the more expensive cuts.

399 Meat (3)

If meat has really 'turned', the only thing you can do is burn it. But if it has only reached the stage of smelling very slightly high, it can be made perfectly edible simply by wiping it over with a clean cloth that has been dipped in vinegar.

400 Meat (4)

Meat, poultry and some fish dishes may be padded out economically by the adding of dried peas, beans, lentils, baked beans, dumplings or pasta.

401 Meat (5)

'Substitute egg for meat' is an old money-saving hint which is still true today.

402 Meat (6)

A meat tenderizer — a wooden or metal mallet with a notched face — pays for itself over and over again. You can use it to turn cheap, tough meat into a delicious repast.

403 Meat (7)

Sausages contain more calories for your money than do mince or beefburgers. Fresh beef or pork sausages are a better buy than canned sausages.

404 Meat (8)

A piece of tough, cheap meat may be made tender by adding a teaspoon of lemon juice to the water in which it is to be cooked. Also, cheaper cuts of meat can be made tender by slow cooking at a low temperature.

405 Meat or poultry left overs

There are three classic ways of using up left over meat or poultry : (a) Serve cold with a salad. (b) Make into rissoles (see no. 394). (c) Make into a quick casserole. (The easy way to do this, if you have no gravy or stock available, is to use a canned soup. When reheating previously cooked meat, be sure to let it simmer for a short while.) For casserole, see nos. 300–305.

406 Milk (1)
Use milk powder for cooking and fresh milk for drinking.

407 Milk (2)
In hot weather, put a pinch of bicarbonate into your milk. It will not go sour so quickly. Milk should also be stood in a cool place, half in a bowl of water, in the dark. (Light, as well as heat, sours milk.)

408 Mince
Some supermarkets are now selling packets of mince mixed with TVP (textured vegetable protein). TVP looks like ordinary mince and is just as nutritious. When it's mixed as 25% TVP to 75% mince, and cooked, no-one can tell the difference. Yet this mixture is considerably cheaper – usually about 80% of the normal price for mince.

409 Mousse (serves four)
Make a jelly. Leave until cool. Whisk in small can of well chilled evaporated milk. Continue to whisk until frothy. Leave to set. Produces a good mousse very much more cheaply than can be bought at the supermarket.

410 Mushrooms (1)
Buy a large quantity of fresh mushrooms in summer or autumn, when the price is lowest. Either freeze them in the freezer or *sauté* lightly and store in the freezing compartment of the fridge.

411 Mushrooms (2)
If you skin mushrooms, you are partially wasting them. Use with skin.

412 Mustard
It would be interesting to know what proportion of mustard is eaten and what proportion is thrown away because it has gone hard. You can prevent mustard from going hard by adding a pinch of table salt when mixing the powder and water. Also, mustard mixed with milk instead of water will never turn dark and remains fresh longer.

413 Mustard and cress
Very good to grow in old plastic margarine containers. If you plant twice per week, you will have a permanent supply.

414 Orange squash
Ingredients: 4 large oranges; 3 lb sugar; $\frac{1}{2}$ gram tartaric

acid; 1 gram citric acid; $\frac{1}{4}$ gram Epsom salts; 2 pints boiling water. Sieve sugar in bowl. Skin oranges and grate the rind into bowl with sugar. Squeeze on the orange juice. Chop up remaining orange pulp and add. Pour on the boiling water, tartaric and citric acids and Epsom salts. Stir. Stand overnight. Drain off solids. Dilute to taste.

415 Parsley
Parsley may be kept fresh for two weeks if stored in a screw-top glass jar with a wide mouth.

416 Pasta
Pasta, which is made from wheat, is an inexpensive and nutritious means of bulking out a meal which does not really contain as much fish, meat or poultry as it might. The reason for the many sizes and shapes is to provide different ways of absorbing different sauces. Thus, spaghetti or spaghettini has no bore and is best in a thick sauce which it absorbs only from the outside. Zitoni (or large bore macaroni) is best with a thin sauce which it can absorb both inside and outside. Seashell shapes not only soak up the sauce from both sides, they also hold it in their inner pockets. Flat pasta, such as lasagne, are best for casseroles. Vermicelli combines well with anchovies and other fish. Noodles are a form of pasta which contain eggs and, therefore, are especially nourishing. (If you invest in an Italian cook-book, it will open up a whole new world of good, cheap food.)

417 Pastes – meat and fish
You can prolong the life of meat or fish paste, once the jar has been opened, by levelling the surface of the paste and pouring on a teaspoonful of melted butter. This reseals the paste against the air.

418 Pâté
If you have a freezer, never throw away poultry livers. Assuming that you do not like giblet pie (which is a fairly safe assumption for most people), keep your poultry livers in the freezer until you have enough to make pâté.

419 Pea-pods
Ever tried pea-pod soup? It's delicious. Instead of throwing the pods away, chop up small, put in a large pan and cover with water. Place on lid and simmer for 1 hour. Strain off solids. Add a chicken stock cube to the liquid.

420 Peas
Why spend extra on garden peas when you can get exactly the same taste from processed peas which have been drained, placed in a casserole with a sprinkle of mint and a little butter, and left in a warm oven for 15 minutes?

421 Pet food (1)
Some kennels sell cat or dog food in bulk. It's the same as you buy in your local supermarket except that it costs about half as much per oz.

422 Pet food (2)
If you have a cat or dog with a taste for fish, try him on sprats bought loose. They are cheaper than tinned pet foods.

423 Pie and flan filling
Cheap bacon pieces, well chopped, make a tasty filling for pies and flans.

424 Pig's head
Pig's head, roasted, is a money-saver. The meat can be cut into chunks and used in stews, curries or 'sweet and sour'. The brains, tongue and other odd pieces, of course, make brawn.

425 Popcorn
Popcorn is quite inexpensive to buy but is still cheaper if you make your own. A small amount of corn blows up in cooking to an enormous size. You can make it sweet (sugared) or savoury (salted) as you wish. It is just the thing for children's parties or as an evening's TV nibble instead of more expensive crisps.

426 Potatoes (1)
Don't believe that myth about potatoes being fattening. Potatoes have fewer calories than Cheddar cheese, lamb chop, bread, fried onions, grilled steak and cream crackers. Furthermore, apart from carbohydrates (for short-term energy and warmth), they contain vitamins B and C, iron and some protein. They are good, cheap food and there are dozens of delicious potato dishes. Write to the *Potato Marketing Board, 50 Hans Crescent, London SW.*

427 Potatoes (2)
Most of the nourishment in a potato is in – or just under – the skin. When you throw away the peelings you throw

away the best part. Get maximum nourishment for your money by leaving the peel where it is. If you don't like jacket potatoes, scrub your potatoes clean, then boil them in their skins and serve with butter. Or, if the skins are very thick, part boil the potatoes, slice them into thick slices and fry.

428 Potatoes (3)
If you *must* remove the peel from new potatoes, and if you have no intention of mincing the peelings (see no. 259), do so by rubbing with a wire pot-scourer – it's quicker than scraping and it leaves you with more potato.

429 Protein
An omelette made with 2 eggs and 1 oz of cheese contains the same protein, but costs half as much, as a serving of roast beef.

430 Prunes
When plums are cheap, make your own prunes! Place some ripe plums, stalks upwards, in a shallow wooden box, cover with paper and leave in a warm place – like an airing cupboard – initially for 24 hours. Then, whenever the oven has been used for cooking, pop the box into the still warm (but unlit) oven, leaving the door open. You will find that the plums gradually shrink. As they do so, arrange them closer together. When they have eventually dried into prunes, pack them in air-tight jars.

431 Pudding padding
Stale bread, sponge cake and biscuit crumbs can all be used successfully to make the main ingredients in puddings, pies, fish and meat dishes go further.

432 Pulses
Much neglected in Britain, beans, peas and lentils are high-calorie foods which also contain vitamin D and plenty of roughage to guard against stomach disorders. There are many dishes from all over the world which use pulses in imaginative and tasty ways to provide good, inexpensive protein. If slimming is a problem for you, simply cut down the quantity of pulse, but do not exclude it altogether. (Most foods that are worth eating have some fattening effect.) The answer is to eat whatever you like, but not excessively, and to take plenty of exercise. The cheapest way to buy pulses is to get them from small

foodshops in immigrant areas, particularly Indian or Italian.

433 Quince jelly and wine
Do you have a Japonica or flowering quince (*Chaenomeles*) in the garden? If so, what do you do with its iron-hard fruit? They make excellent jelly or wine. Also, if you peel them, remove the core and cut into slices; they mix well with apples in a pie or fruit stew.

434 Rice and lentil roll
Ingredients: equal parts cooked rice and lentils, (soak lentils overnight before cooking); olive oil; young tender cabbage leaves; tomato juice from tin of tomatoes. Blend the rice and lentils into a paste. Add a little olive oil. Gently boil cabbage leaves until soft. Wrap the leaves around rice-lentil mixture and fashion into rolls with 1 leaf per roll. Tie with cotton to keep roll secure. Place in tomato juice and heat gently for 10 minutes.

435 Rice pudding
Add a pinch of bicarbonate of soda to rice and your rice pudding will cook more quickly.

436 Salads
Don't throw away celery tops. Chopped up small, they improve a salad. So do plantain, dandelion and nasturtium leaves. Dandelion leaves can also be boiled rapidly in salted water until tender. Drain. Serve cold with olive oil and lemon juice dressing.

437 Salmon substitute
Bar or dog fish (don't be put off by the name!) can be used successfully in any recipes in place of salmon.

438 Salt
Don't fall into the error of using table salt for cooking. Instead, buy cooking salt in a large block for cheapness. Grate with a coarse grater and keep in an air-tight container.

439 Sandwich spread (1)
Don't forget the good old bread and dripping, beloved in the North of England. Blend together various fat drippings. Spread on bread. Add salt to taste.

440 Sandwich spread (2)
Another job for the mincer: if you have any hard, dried-up

cheese, toss it in along with an onion. Result: a tasty sandwich spread.

441 Sauce
End of the bottle? Stand it in a bowl of really hot water for a few seconds, then pour out the dregs. Or rinse out with a small amount of hot water and pour into your casserole or rissole mix – or new bottle of sauce.

442 Sausages
Don't buy sausages, buy sausage meat. It saves several p. per pound – and what's so special about sausage skin?

443 Scones
Scones should normally be eaten fresh. But if you still have some of yesterday's, fry in butter and, if sweet, serve with honey or jam; if savoury, top with fried egg.

444 Shellfish
The limpets which cling to seashore rocks (and are ignored by almost everyone) have an excellent flavour and could be substituted for oysters in many dishes. (Be sure not to take them from polluted waters.)

445 Snacks before meals
Many families fall into the bad habit of eating between meals. This can waste money in two ways. Firstly, the things that people eat between meals – biscuits, cakes, sweets, etc. – are themselves very expensive in terms of nourishment per p. spent. Secondly, they kill the appetite so that good, nourishing food that has been prepared for a main meal is sometimes left on the plate, uneaten. If people *must* eat between meals, it is more sensible to nibble a carrot or some fruit, or drink milk or a bowl of soup, rather than a heap of stodge which is good for nothing but destroying the waistline. If they do this, however, their next meal should be made slightly smaller to avoid wastage.

446 Snack from left overs
Old, rejected sandwiches look very sad. Cheer them up by coating in batter (see no. 270). Fry and serve hot.

447 Soft fruit (1)
If your garden is not very large, loganberries or blackberries are the best crop because they give the highest yield of fruit per square foot.

448 Soft fruit (2)
Don't overlook the free fruit in the hedgerows. Blackberry jam, rosehip syrup, elderberry syrup or hazel nuts for the cake can all result from an enjoyable day in the country.

449 Soup (1)
Left over gravy and vegetables, liquidised and heated to boiling point, make a good soup.

450 Soup (2)
Nettles make excellent soup – and there are plenty of them about, free. Wear gloves to pick them! Pluck the nettle tops and also the small, young shoots. Wash well in salted water and chop small. Boil water with a chicken stock cube. Add nettles and finely chopped potatoes and cook until thick.

451 Soups – packet
Large size packet soups, as sold by the freezer food stores and some of the supermarkets, are much more economical than canned ones.

452 Soup stock (1)
Pour left over gravy and vegetable juices into plastic ice-cube trays and keep in the freezer to produce ready-made stock cubes which are conveniently broken down into small quantities.

453 Soup stock (2)
Chicken bones and giblets, crushed and mixed together in the blender, make delicious and nourishing stock for soup.

454 Soup stock (3)
A good stock for soups can be made from bacon rind ($\frac{1}{2}$ lb rind makes a quart of stock). Remove the rind from the bacon with scissors. Put in a saucepan and cover with boiling water. After 5 minutes, drain off the hot water and replace with cold. Bring to the boil and simmer for 1 hour. Most vegetable 'waste' – like celery roots or cabbage or lettuce leaves – can be made into nourishing stock. But beware of rhubarb leaves – they are highly poisonous.

455 Spices
An inexpensive packet of pickling spice contains a variety of peppercorns, ginger, bay leaves, mustard

seeds, pimento, cloves, etc., from which you may pick and choose to suit the dish you are preparing. You will find this much cheaper than buying spices individually.

456 Spinach omelette

Soak $\frac{1}{2}$ loaf of bread — stale bread will do — overnight in cold water. Prepare 2 cups of cooked spinach *purée* (well drained). Take 2 large eggs and mix into the spinach. Mix in $\frac{1}{4}$ cup of grated cheese. Bind this mixture with the soaked bread. Grease a casserole dish and pour in mixture. Sprinkle another $\frac{1}{4}$ cup of grated cheese on top. Cook in slow oven until omelette begins to rise — then drop temperature and bake in slow oven for about $\frac{1}{2}$ hour or until cooked. Cut into squares and serve.

457 Spinach substitute (1)

Nettles (would you believe?) are as tasty and nutritious as spinach — and they're free! All you need is a good pair of gloves. Pick the young, tender nettles. Wash well in salted water, still wearing the gloves. Cook in just a few tablespoons of water with a knob of butter, salt and pepper. The result is a delicious *purée*, very like spinach.

458 Spinach substitute (2)

Radish, beet and turnip tops and dandelion leaves can all be served like spinach, too.

459 Steak

A slice of bread served under a steak gives it much greater self confidence by making it look and feel taller. It also helps the taste of the steak and fills up the eater.

460 Suet

Always buy your lambs' kidneys with the fat on, if you can — that fat is the best quality suet. Grate it and store for use in puddings or stuffing.

461 Suet puddings

Do you buy a packet of suet when you want to make a winter pudding? Butcher's suet is a fraction of the price.

462 Sugar (1)

As a nation, we are sugar-crazy. Sugar is not only bad for your heart and teeth, it costs far too much and its over-use ruins other, more delicate flavours in many a dish. It is well worth the effort to cut down your intake of sugar. If you simply cannot take your cuppa unsweetened, try substituting (or subsidising) with one of the branded saccharin products (available in both tablet and powder form).

463 Sugar (2)
It is a fact that, when the sugar bowl is half empty, people do take smaller spoon loads than when it is full. So, make sure you only half fill the sugar bowl.

464 Sugar (3)
Reduce the recommended sugar content by 1 oz when making biscuits, custards and puddings. But not when making cakes — it would spoil their texture and volume.

465 Sugar/flour
Distrust all paper bags which contain sugar and flour: they have a mean way of keeping back several grammes, hiding them within their folds. You can foil them by cutting open the lower end when they are supposed to be empty and giving them a good shake.

466 Sugar for jam
When making jam in wartime, we used to economise on sugar by using 1 teaspoon glycerine and only ¾ lb sugar (instead of 1 lb) to each 1 lb of fruit.

467 Sugar for stewed fruit (1)
Save sugar in two ways when stewing fruit. First, if you add ¼ oz bicarbonate to each pound of fruit, you can halve the usual amount of sugar. Second, sugar will go even further if added during the last 5 minutes or so of cooking.

468 Sugar for stewed fruit (2)
Another way of economising on sugar when stewing high acid fruits is to use 1 pint of water, 2 heaped tablespoons flaked tapioca — and only 1 heaped tablespoon sugar — for every ½ lb fruit. Bring to the boil and cook on a moderate heat for 10–15 minutes.

469 Tea (1)
A packet of tea will go much further in this way: place a fine-mesh strainer over the top of your cup; put a spoon of tea in the strainer and pour boiling water through it until the cup is full. If left for a few seconds, you will find that the same tea and strainer will provide an excellent second and third cup of tea. Making tea in the normal way,

in a tea-pot, you might have used three or four spoons of tea to obtain the same result.

470 Tea (2)
Forget tea-bags — they are much more expensive than packeted tea.

471 Tea (3)
Never mind the 'one for the pot' — just let it brew a little longer!

472 Tea (4)
An excellent digestive tea can be made from dried, wild mint.

473 Tea (5)
Clover is plentiful and makes a good tea. Chop up 1 oz of clover plant, including both flower and leaves. Pour 1 pint boiling water on to the clover and leave for 5 minutes. Strain and serve like tea.

474 Tea (6)
Try adding a blackcurrant leaf to the cheapest, most nodescript brand of tea that you can buy. The blackcurrant leaf adds a touch of fragrance and class which one normally finds only in an expensive blend.

475 Tea (7)
You can use fewer spoonsful of tea and still get the same strength by spreading the tea-leaves on a piece of tinfoil in a warm oven for ten minutes before use. (But only do this if the oven is already in use!)

476 Tomato sauce (1)
Buy about 2 lb of cheap, squashy tomatoes from the market. Liquidise to make 1 pint of juice. Finely chop up 1 large onion and add to the tomato juice with salt, pepper, lemon juice and Worcester sauce to taste. Cook until the onion is really soft. Strain. Keep in fridge.

477 Tomato sauce (2)
Economise on tomatoes by slipping apple and/or swede into the above mix.

478 Tuna fish
To get the full flavour, flake with a fork, sprinkle with salt and vinegar and leave standing for four hours. (If you do this, your tuna will be as tasty as salmon!)

479 Trifle topping

A satisfactory topping for a jelly or trifle can be made by whipping evaporated milk. First, boil the unopened tin of milk in a pan of water for 30 minutes. Remove from tin, allow to cool and put into the fridge for an hour. Whisk with a fork.

480 Tripe

Tripe is an extremely nourishing and easily digested food, as well as being quite cheap. Unfortunately, it needs long, slow cooking – but it is still a cheap meal, despite the fuel required. Because it doesn't have much flavour of its own, tripe needs to have a stronger taste, such as onions, combined with it.

481 Vegetables – left overs

The three most popular ways of using up vegetables are: (a) Put them into salads. (b) Add to a stew towards the end of cooking (but not green vegetables, of course). (c) Make into bubble and squeak. (Mix equal parts mashed potato and cooked, chopped green vegetable, like cabbage. Blend into an even texture. Add salt and pepper. Heat 2 oz fat in frying pan. Put mixture into pan and flatten with knife. Cook on slow heat until golden brown underneath. Turn over mixture and cook other side.)

482 Vegetables – mixed

An inexpensive, yet tasty, blend of vegetables may be obtained by chopping and mixing together carrot, onion and celery.

483 Vinegar

Why not make your own? Put all apple waste (skins and cores) in a large container with just enough cold water to cover. Keep adding apple waste and cold water from time to time. Always keep jar covered with muslin or netting and stand in warm place. A crust will form on the top. Sample the vinegar at intervals for taste and smell. When strong enough, remove crust. Sieve vinegar to remove all solids. Bottle. Cork.

484 Wine (1)

If you are an enthusiastic wine drinker, you will save a lot of money by making your own. There are many books on the subject, along with kits for home wine-making.

485 Wine (2)
If making your own wine is too much trouble, the cheapest way to buy is by the barrel. Enquire at your wine shop. If the cost is too much, ask your wine-drinking friends to share the expense and the barrel. You would then bottle your own.

486 Wine for cooking (1)
You can halve the amount of wine needed without harming the flavour of the finished dish by substituting 50% freshly made tea.

487 Wine for cooking (2)
Instead of wine, try cider or beer when cooking meat, fish and poultry.

488 Yoghurt
Yoghurt is a nutritious food that costs very little; that can be varied in flavour to suit anyone; that is excellent for slimmers; that you can make easily. You need a warm bowl, a plate, a sieve, a tea-towel, a spoon and a carton of plain yoghurt (which may be a bought one). Leave the yoghurt out of fridge until it is at room temperature (probably 3 or 4 hours). Heat 1 pint of milk but do *not* allow to boil. Allow milk to cool until it feels just warm to the inside of your wrist. Pour milk through sieve into warm bowl and stir in a heaped tablespoon of yoghurt. Place plate on top of bowl and wrap warm towel around the whole. Leave in warm place – such as near the central heating boiler – for about 8 hours. When you unwrap, you will find that you have a bowl of yoghurt. Chill. Keep some to start the next batch. Mix the remainder with soft fruit or jam, to taste.

How to save money on
Fuel

489   Baking (1)
Have a weekly 'bake-in', filling the oven to capacity. (For bread baking, see no. 278.) Then keep your week's supply in a tin or a freezer.

490   Baking (2)
Buying a new electric oven? If you do a lot of baking, consider the fan oven, which extracts the maximum usage from the minimum electricity by circulating the heat.

491   Central heating (1)
If you are having domestic central heating installed, the Heating and Ventilating Contractors' Association guarantees the standard of work done by their HVCA members. And if any of their members default, the Association will help you. Write or telephone: *Heating and Ventilating Contractors' Association, Home Heating Group, 172 Buckingham Palace Road, London SW1 W9TD (01-730 8245)*.

Advice about the most suitable heating system for your home is also available (for a small fee) from the *National Heating Consultancy, 188 Albany Street, London, NW1 4AP (01-388 0862)*.

To help you choose the solid fuel heating appliance best suited to your home and pocket, contact the Solid Fuel Advisory Service (which combines the vast knowledge of The National Coal Board, Coalite, Rexco and the coal merchants, including the Co-op). It also advises on the most suitable solid fuels and how to pay for them economically. This service is available at more than 70 offices throughout the country. Write to the following address to find your nearest advice centre: *The Solid Fuel Advisory Service, The National Coal Board, Hobart House, Grosvenor Place, London SW1X 7AE*.

492   Central heating (2)
When central heating running costs for the various fuels are compared, there is one point which is sometimes over-

looked. Although a solid fuel boiler is easily the cheapest to run, it has the disadvantage that it uses fuel all the time just to stay alight. And when the house is empty all day, this does seem rather wasteful when compared with the fuels which may be easily controlled by thermostats.

493 Central heating (3)

It is sad that many people, having had central heating for only a short time, can now barely afford to turn it on, because of the excessively high fuel costs. One answer is to try to confine one's use of the house to the minimum number of rooms, so that fewer rooms need full heating. (Enough heat should be maintained to prevent condensation forming.)

494 Central heating (4)

If you have full central heating, consider the advantages of adding extra time switches and thermostats to individual radiators. This would save fuel by enabling you to have the heat where and when you want it.

With any central heating system, there is a natural tendency to leave it on and forget about it. Don't! Always remember that a central heating system needs about 10% more fuel to raise the temperature 3° F. Whether it operates on electricity, gas, oil or solid fuel – it's really money that you're burning. Set the boiler or room thermostat to maintain an acceptable level; 63° F should be enough.

495 Central heating (5)

Make sure that your radiators are not surrounded by furniture. This is bad for the heating efficiency and bad for the furniture.

496 Central heating (6)

Set the time clock on your central heating system to bring radiators into operation as late as possible in the morning (without being uncomfortably cool on rising). Set it to switch off your radiators one hour before bed-time. A warm air installation may need to be left on a little longer.

497 Central heating (7)

Always draw your curtains at night when the radiators are on. Heavy curtains are almost as effective as double glazing. But make sure that no curtains hang over radiators or heat will escape.

498 Central heating – gas
Lower thermostat settings to the minimum if you are going away from home for more than two days. Turn them up when you return.

499 Cooking (1)
Although some recipes tell you to 'place in a warm oven', it is nevertheless true that most foods cook just as well from a cold start. So why waste time and fuel ?

500 Cooking (2)
Don't use your oven in fits and starts. Plan your cooking so as to always have an oven full of food.

501 Cooking (3)
If you are cooking, say, fish and vegetables, you can save fuel. While cooking the vegetables in a saucepan, place an enamel or earthenware dish containing the fish into the saucepan, on top of the vegetables. Then use the saucepan lid to cover the dish. In this way, the one plate or ring will cook both foods.

502 Cooking (4)
If you have an electric cooker, try not to waste the excess heat which hangs around after switching off. Such jobs as drying bread or heating a lemon before squeezing (see no. 384) can be done entirely in a cooling oven. Most dishes can be finished in a switched off electric oven.

503 Cooking (5)
If your gas cooker has cast iron burner caps, place a square sheet of iron upon a hot gas ring and it will keep three or four pots boiling simultaneously. But do not try this if your cooker's burner caps are aluminium or they will deform.

504 Cooking (6)
When baking potatoes in the oven, put them on to a metal skewer. Because the skewer itself is such a good heat conductor, it bakes the potatoes *from the inside*. Thus, they are ready in less than half the normal time.

505 Cooking (7)
Always measure the correct amount of water into the kettle so that you do not waste fuel by boiling more than is needed.

506 Cooking (8)
Be sure to use enough water to cook the food without

needing to top up. Adding cold water part way through the cooking process merely wastes fuel.

507 Cooking (9)
Pans should completely cover the hot plates of electric cookers. Gas flames should not be allowed to creep up the sides of the pans as this wastes fuel.

508 Cooking (10)
A large vacuum flask can also save your cooking fuel. Such foods as stews, rice, meat and root vegetables should be first brought to the boil and then poured into the flask where they will continue to cook satisfactorily. You will need to experiment with the timing.

509 Cooking (11)
Similarly, instead of a vacuum flask, you can make a wooden box lined with polystyrene ceiling tiles and large enough to contain cloth pads filled with hay or chaff on all sides (including the top). Boil the food in a vessel with a tight-fitting lid. Place vessel (with lid) into the insulated box, covering it with the top pad before closing the lid. The food will continue to cook gently as long as enclosed.

510 Cooking (12)
Lids on pans save moisture during cooking and heat after cooking. (But don't leave a lid on rice after it has cooked.)

511 Cooking (13)
Have you thought of purchasing a set of those three triangular saucepans which fit together into a circle and use only one burner? If they are of the right size for your family cooking, they would eventually pay for themselves in saved fuel.

512 Cooking (14)
If you have an oven which switches itself off, set it to do this even though you are staying in the house. This will ensure that you do not overcook food – or waste fuel – for even a second.

513 Cooking (15)
Never cook with a half empty oven if you can possibly avoid it. Potatoes baked in their jackets are a useful way of filling up the oven. Besides the casserole (or roast) and potatoes, you could have root vegetables in a little water, salt and butter/margarine, plus a baked sweet.

514   Cooking (16)
If you own a double oven cooker, be mean with yourself
and try to use only one – packed to capacity – rather than
have both on at the same time.

515   Cooking by gas
As soon as a pan boils, turn the gas as low as possible.
Cooking will continue, even on a tiny flame.

516   Cooking by pressure cooker
A pressure cooker is a fine money-saver. If you have one,
use it. It enables several things to be cooked together and
also shortens cooking time.

517   Cooking by steamer
A steamer may be used to cook two lots of vegetables, one
above the other, at the same time. Or try vegetables and
steam puddings one on top of the other. Small 'individual'
steam puddings, made in cups, cook more rapidly than
one large pudding. If you don't have a steamer, use a metal
colander over a saucepan.

518   Cooking by vacuum jars
Vacuum jars can save your fuel. For example, place prunes
or apricots in a vacuum jar and cover with boiled water
from the kettle. Tighten the lid and leave overnight. Next
morning, the fruit will be cooked. (You can also part-cook
a stew on a cooker and let a pre-heated vacuum jar finish it
off in two or three hours.)

519   Cooking potatoes (1)
Boiling potatoes can take a lot of expensive fuel and
produce a very dull vegetable. Try this method instead : Cut
potatoes into tiny cubes. Put in saucepan with a little milk
and a knob of butter or margarine. Put lid on pan. Cook for
five to ten minutes. Add salt and pepper. Mash.

520   Cooking potatoes (2)
If you soak jacket potatoes in salt water before cooking
them, they will save fuel by baking more quickly.

521   Cooking vegetables (1)
When boiling vegetables, don't drown them (it spoils the
flavour and wastes fuel) and don't boil them too long (it
kills the vitamins and wastes fuel). Cut them small, so that
they will cook evenly and quickly. Then give them the
minimum water and just enough cooking to make them

tender enough to eat. And don't throw away the water — it's full of vitamins. Use for stock. Grated vegetables — particularly onions — cook much more rapidly (and use far less fuel) than finely chopped vegetables.

522 Cooking vegetables (2)
Cook more than one type of vegetable in a pan at the same time, so long as they are vegetables which take the same time to cook. If you wish, you can keep them apart from each other by wrapping in tinfoil.

523 Dishwasher — electric
If you have an electric dishwasher, it is worth investing in extra crockery so that you can put the dirty dishes from all the meals straight into the washer only once per day, in the evening, thus saving time and electricity.

524 Drying the washing
Never use a drying cabinet when there's free sunshine in the back garden. And never use a drying cabinet if you have a warm odour-free kitchen after cooking a meal. (In fact, it is possible to learn to live without a drying cabinet, especially if your house has radiators.)

525 Electrical appliances — general
You buy electricity in units of 'kilowatt hours'. This means that, if electricity in your area costs, say, 1p per kilowatt hour, a 60-watt light bulb could burn for 16 hours 40 minutes for 1p (bearing in mind that there are 1000 watts in 1 kilowatt — $1000 \div 60 = 16\frac{2}{3}$). Or a 3-kilowatt heater would burn away your money at a rate of 3p per hour. Have you considered converting to a white meter? This costs slightly *more* during the day, but considerably less at night. Charges vary from one electricity board to another, but in many areas white meter electricity is only marginally dearer during the day, but less than half the normal rate between the hours of 9.00 pm and 7.00 am, which is when most electricity is needed. If you have a white meter it pays to keep these times constantly in mind. (Caution! The night rate times vary from area to area, so you need to check these — and also the rates — with your local electricity board.)

Get into the habit of thinking in terms of so many pence per hour for different electrical appliances. It is as well to have some idea of where one's money is going. Here are a few guidelines:

A 3-kilowatt electric oven or immersion heater uses the same electricity in 20 minutes as:
A 1-bar (1-kilowatt) fire in 1 hour.
A colour TV set in 3½ hours.
A black and white TV set in 10 hours.
A vacuum cleaner in 2–4 hours (depending on size).
A portable drill in 4½ hours.
1 100-watt light bulb in 10 hours.

The Electrical Association for Women is willing to give information concerning electrical equipment in the home and will answer queries regarding the use of electricity. *The Electrical Association for Women, 25 Fouberts Place, London W1V 2AL (01-437 5212).*

526 Electric blanket (1)

You don't need to use an electric blanket if you: (a) Have a warm bed which is properly insulated. (Continental quilts are the best because they are both warm and light.) (b) Wear bed socks, which can be knitted out of old, unpicked woollen garments. (c) Spend the first few minutes in bed with your head under the covers so that your warm breath generates heat inside the bed.

527 Electric blanket (2)

If you *must* use an electric blanket, put an extra bed blanket beneath the bottom sheet – it will help to keep the warmth in.

528 Electric iron (1)

Excessive ironing is a waste of electricity. There is no real need to iron pyjamas, tea-towels, bed sheets, pillow cases or most underclothing. Just pull them into shape while drying and then, when thoroughly dry, fold and put away. Any slight creases in pyjamas or underclothing are removed by the warmth of the body within five minutes of putting them on. It is a good ploy to use an over-large undersheet on the bed. Tie a knot in each corner and tuck them underneath the mattress. This will pull the unironed sheet taut and smooth.

529 Electric iron (2)

Should you wish to iron bedding, do so by laying the large, flat articles – like folded sheets or pillowcases – over the ironing board before you start. Then iron small articles on top of them, thus dealing with several layers at once.

530 Electricity – complaints
Only specific complaints, please – not general moanings and groanings about the high cost of electricity. First, contact the manager of your local electricity board. Then, if not satisfied, refer the matter to the Secretary of the Electricity Consultative Council – the address is usually given on the back of each bill or on a display notice at the electricity board showroom.

531 Electricity – water heating
Electricity is at its most costly when used to give heat, especially heat to water. Therefore, you could make a long-term saving by installing a one- to three-gallon water heater over the sink. Do not believe people who tell you that immersion heaters are more economical left on all day. If you do this, your electricity bill will be much higher than by using the immersion heater for half an hour morning and evening. Of course, the hot water tank and pipes need to be very well lagged to keep in the heat. So, if the water is not quite as hot as you would like it, do not work the heater any harder – pay more attention to insulation.

532 Electric kettles, washing machines, water heaters
In a hard water area, it will profit you to spend a little money on a descaling powder, which will enable kettles, washing machines and small water heaters to work more efficiently and use less fuel.

533 Fluorescent lights
If you know that you will be going in and out of the kitchen several times during the next hour, it is wasteful to keep switching the fluorescent light on and off. So much electricity is needed to light it up each time that it is better to leave it on. Also, the tube will last longer.

534 Foot warmer for bed
Older people have great difficulty in keeping their feet warm in bed. One of the simplest, cheapest and most effective remedies is to wrap an old nylon nightdress around the feet (but take care when getting out of bed – don't forget the nightdress is there!).

535 Freezer
Your food freezer should be kept at least three-quarters full for maximum fuel economy.

536 Gas – buying (1)
If your usage of gas is high and you have a pre-payment meter, you could save a lot of money by changing to a credit meter. Ask for details at your local gas board show-room.

537 Gas – buying (2)
Each gas region has several different tariffs. Which one you should be on depends upon your area and your own usage. Check with your regional office.

538 Gas – complaints
If you have a particular problem concerning gas (not a general grouse about charges), first tell the manager of your local gas board. If he can't help, write to the Secretary of the Gas Consumer Council, the address of which may be found on the back of a bill or on a display notice at the gas board showroom.

539 Gas – pilot light (1)
If you have a gas cooker with a pilot light, turn it off – and save yourself about £8 per year. Even if you use matches, you won't use £8 worth! A battery operated lighter will work for a year on a battery costing much less than £1.

540 Gas – pilot light (2)
If you feel you *must* keep your pilot light ablaze, at least make it work for you by leaving a kettle of water on it overnight. Next morning, tea can be made more quickly – and economically. You can do the same during the day.

541 Gas pokers
Don't leave gas pokers in too long when starting a fire – it only wastes gas and wears out the poker. (A few sticks will reduce kindling time.)

542 Hot water
When making tea, it is not an economy to put hot water from the tap into the kettle (in the belief that it will need less heating to reach boiling point). Replacing the hot water drawn from the tank costs more than boiling cold water in a kettle.

543 Household cleaning
Save the hot, soapy water from your twin-tub washing machine or electrical boiler in a bucket for household cleaning jobs.

544 Lighting (1)
Localised lighting enables you to have the most light where it will be of the greatest use – and it's more economical than high-powered, general lighting.

545 Lighting (2)
Coloured or decorative lampshades reduce light output drastically. A lampshade should soften and diffuse light, not obscure it. Change to plain, white lampshades. If the light is brighter than needed, use a bulb of lower wattage.

546 Lighting (3)
Use fluorescent lighting wherever you can reasonably do so. A 40-watt fluorescent lamp gives as much light as a 150-watt bulb. It is particularly suitable for kitchens or anywhere else where a lot of light is needed.

547 Lighting (4)
You should not view TV in a totally darkened room – it's bad for the eyes. But neither need you view with the main room light on – it's a waste of electricity. A small, low-wattage table lamp on the TV is sufficient. Alternatively, you could fit a dimmer switch which enables you to turn down the main room light to the required level – and use less power.

548 Oil – buying
Find out from your supplier whether he will give you quantity discounts. Sometimes these are possible, providing your tank will take at least 1000 gallons.

549 Plate warming
Put heatproof plates in the oven when in use instead of heating them separately, afterwards.

550 Refrigerator
Let warm food go cold before putting it in the fridge.

551 Refrigerators/freezers (1)
De-frost refrigerators and freezers with absolute regularity, according to the manufacturers' instructions. A build-up of ice wastes electricity.

552 Refrigerators/freezers (2)
Never open the door of your fridge or freezer unnecessarily ; put in or take out quickly and get the door closed again as soon as possible.

553 Solid Fuel (1)
If you have a solid fuel boiler, always sieve the ashes for unburnt fuel.

554 Solid fuel (2)
Place large pieces of coal with the grain running horizontally – they will burn longer.

555 Solid fuel (3)
Don't waste loose coal dust. Shovel it into paper bags and then wrap in a newspaper. When it is placed on the fire, the dust will cake together and burn like coal – but do not poke or disturb it! Those funny shaped egg-boxes, when filled with coal dust, watered and dried, make excellent long-burning coal bricks.

556 Solid fuel (4)
Alternatively, coal bricks can be made as follows: Mix 10 parts of coal slack with one part of cement. Add a little water – just enough to make into a thick paste. Pour into any mould of a suitable size – e.g. a flower pot or small wooden box. Allow to dry hard. When on the fire, do not poke.

557 Solid fuel (5)
Another way to make coal bricks is to mix two parts of coal dust with one part of sawdust. Add water which has had a cold-water glue added. Shape into eggs or bricks. Allow to dry. Do not poke when on the fire.

558 Solid fuel (6)
The cheapest coal bricks of all are made by mixing coal dust with garden soil. Pack into old paper bags and leave in the garden shed until hard. Again, do not poke when burning.

559 Solid fuel (7)
Sprinkle coal with a mixture of one teaspoon of soda to two quarts of water and let dry before use. It will burn longer and cleaner.

560 Solid fuel – buying
Shop around and buy in large quantity (over one ton).

561 Solid fuel – coal: complaints
Write to the *Domestic Coal Consumers' Council, Thames House South, Millbank, London SW1,* and ask for the

name and address of the Regional Secretary for your area of the Approved Coal Merchants Scheme.

562   Space heating (1)
If your need is for just a few (say, five) hours' heating per day, probably the cheapest form would be a paraffin heater – either radiant or convector. (Solid fuel in an open grate is inefficient because so much of the heat is lost up the chimney.)

563   Space heating (2)
If you have a room-heater sealed into the fireplace, make sure that the seal is a perfect one; if it is cracked or loose, warm air will be drawn straight up the chimney.

564   Space heating (3)
Dampness is not only unhealthy, it also uses up heat. So you should cure it in the interests of economy.

565   Space heating (4)
Never let a room get so hot that you must open a window. If you are going to throw a party to a roomful of people, do not make the mistake of having the room too warm to start with. People give out heat and a large number of people give out a lot of heat.

566   Space heating (5)
Keep doors closed, especially of unused rooms.

567   Space heating (6)
The performance of a portable electric fire can be greatly improved by building a three-sided heat reflector to stand behind it, like a screen. Use asbestos board and cover it completely with aluminium kitchen foil. Design it to about double the height of your fire. You will find that heat is so boosted that, frequently, only one bar of a two-bar fire is needed, thus saving electricity.

568   Space heating (7)
One can save considerable sums of money upon expensive space heating by dressing warmly. A string vest worn under warm clothing (as when skiing) can save you a lot of fuel.

569   Space heating – insulation: assessment
In 1974, Applied Research of Cambridge Ltd. ran a computer program on the cost effectiveness of using

different methods of insulation over a 20-year period. The kind of house represented was an average semi-detached with a ground floor area of 50 square metres and an annual fuel bill of £150 before insulation. In the following table, columns 1 and 2 were ARC Report figures. Column 3 has been produced by dividing each Mean Annual Saving by the Initial Cost, thus giving the Mean Annual Savings per Pound Spent – a measurement of how much value you would get for your money.

Type of insulation	1 Initial Cost	2 Mean Annual Saving	3 MAS per Pound Spent
	£	£	£
Weatherstrip draught exclusion	5	11.78	2.36
Weatherstrip + roof insulation (2″ glass fibre)	25	28.84	1.15
Roof insulation (2″ glass fibre)	20	15.05	.75
Weatherstrip + roof insulation + injected foam in walls	100	54.86	.55
Walls (injected foam)	75	32.12	.43
Weatherstrip + roof insulation + insulated walls + double glazing	300	69.79	.23
Weatherstrip + roof insulation + double glazing	225	35.75	.16
Double glazing	200	8.05	.04

Conclusion: You should use weatherstrip and roof insulation immediately and begin to make a sizeable saving quickly and at little cost. If you can afford it, you should also have cavity walls insulated by injected foam. But double glazing is a luxury which you can do without, especially if you have thick curtains.

570 Space heating – insulation: doors and windows
About 15% of the heat you lose goes around the sides of draughty doors and windows. Metal (or foam) strip draught-proofing secured around the frames of all your outside doors costs very little and will save you many pounds per annum in heating costs. The metal ones are a little more difficult to fix, but last much longer. Hinged windows should be draught-proofed with sticky-backed foam plastic strip.

571 Space heating – insulation: fireplace (1)
If you have an open fireplace which is used only occasionally, fit a 'throat restrictor' in the flue, immediately above the grate.

572 Space heating – insulation: fireplace (2)
Prevent cold draughts by blocking off unused fireplaces with hardboard. But don't forget to install an air grille or your chimney will eventually suffer from condensation, which will produce spectacular damp patches on the wallpaper.

573 Space heating – insulation: floor
As much as 15% of your lost heat may go through the gaps between skirting and floorboards. You can stop this with the aid of newspaper, papier mâché or beading, plus, if possible, sheets of hardboard on the floor and a floor covering of your choice.

574 Space heating – insulation: letter-box
Don't forget the letter-box! There's not much point in injected resin foam and double glazing if you have a gale of cold air whistling in through this hole in your front door. You can buy a special anti-draft device quite cheaply from most D-I-Y shops.

575 Space heating – insulation: overflow pipe
When not in use, an overflow pipe from kitchen or bathroom becomes an inflow pipe for cold air. You can save your heating by cutting the end off a balloon and pulling its neck over the outlet pipe, outside. While allowing the water to flow out, this will prevent the cold air blowing in.

576 Space heating – insulation: porch
A storm-proof front porch insulates the whole house and

makes it warmer. It is cheaper to have your porch glazed than to pay heavily on heating.

577 Space heating – insulation: roof
Heat rises. So, about 25% of your lost heat goes straight through the roof. You can stop it by insulating the loft with either 3″-thick rolls of glass fibre or loose-fill. (Better wear gloves!)

Also, lag the cold water tank and the pipes going to it, but *do not* put lagging underneath the tank – if you do you might cut off heat from below which would help to prevent your tank from freezing.

578 Space heating – insulation: underfloor draughts
Newspaper is a very good heat insulator, but *do not* use it for insulating the loft because of the fire risk. Instead, lay it down either underneath or instead of the carpet underfelt. It will help to prevent draughts and also reduce wear on your carpets.

579 Space heating – insulation: walls (1)
Approximately 35% of the heat that is wasted is lost through the walls. If you have cavity walls, the ideal answer is to have them insulated by the injection of resin foam, but this is a job for a specialist firm, and quite expensive. If you decide to have this done, obtain quotations from several firms and make sure that the selected contractor holds an Agréments Certificate (which guarantees the quality of his materials).

580 Space heating – insulation: walls (2)
Much of the heat from a radiator goes straight into the wall, which is rather a waste, particularly if the radiator is standing against an outside wall. You can put this right by glueing or taping a sheet of aluminium kitchen foil (the size of the radiator) to the wall immediately behind the appliance. It will bounce the heat back into the room.

581 Toast – making
A pop-up toaster uses less fuel than a grill to make toast.

582 Washing machine
If you have a launderette within walking distance, it is cheaper to use this than a washing machine of your own. This was the conclusion reached by a recent survey which took into account the full cost of electricity, servicing and depreciation of the machine.

583   Washing machine/launderette
Wait until you have a full load before using the hottest wash.

584   Water heating (1)
A dripping hot water tap is leaking away money. Get it put right as quickly as possible. A tap that drips once per second wastes 300 to 400 gallons of water per year. (The Water Board will replace a worn tap washer free of charge.)

585   Water heating (2)
Never wash your hands under running warm water — it wastes too much. Use the wash basin or, better still, a small bowl in the basin.

586   Water heating (3)
Pre-soaking whites in cold water enables you to get away with a warm wash instead of a hot one, thus saving fuel.

587   Water heating (4)
A shower not only cleans you more efficiently and quickly — it uses less hot water (and fuel) than the average bath.

588   Water heating (5)
Furred up pipes and water heaters are inefficient and waste fuel. You can keep the system scale-free for six months by suspending a special device containing micromet crystals in the cold water tank. With replacement crystals, this will cost less than £3 for a year and, in a hard water area, could save 10% of the fuel bills. For other information write to the *Hard Water Information Bureau, 6 Cavendish Square, London W1M 9HA.*

589   Water heating (6)
A kitchen alarm can save you money! When preparing a meal, switch on the immersion heater and set the alarm for half an hour. Switch off the heater when the alarm goes — you now have enough hot water for dishes.

590   Water heating (7)
When washing by hand or using a twin-tub or wringer machine rinse, use only cold water.

591   Water heating (8)
An old wartime hint for saving fuel was to bathe in only 5″ of water. You can clean yourself perfectly well in this depth.

592 Water heating (9)
Bathe with another member of the family.

593 Water heating – insulation
For around £5 (the cost of a 3″-thick insulating jacket) you can save up to £1 per week by lagging your hot water tank. Therefore, you begin to make a profit after about five weeks. Measure your tank from top to bottom and around its circumference – and then enquire at your gas or electricity showroom, hardware or D-I-Y store.

How to save money on
Gardening

594 Allotments
Ask the Parks Department of your local council whether they are one of the local authorities to have allotments. If so, and you decide to apply for one, you will probably have to go on a waiting list.

Also, join a local gardening association. This would probably cost 25p–50p per annum and membership would enable you to buy seed and fertiliser at discount prices, as well as receiving helpful free advice. Write to the *National Society of Leisure Gardeners Ltd., 22 High Street, Flitwick, Bedfordshire MK45 1DT,* for the address of your nearest association.

595 Cat deterrent
If the ginger tom from next door behaves in an un-neighbourly way towards your garden, there is no need to buy a branded product to discourage him. Try some dried orange and/or lemon peel, crushed to a powder and scattered on his favourite spot.

596 Caterpillar exterminator
For this you need to save up or acquire $\frac{1}{2}$ lb of filter cigarette ends. Boil them in 1 gallon of water for $\frac{1}{2}$ hour. Drain. Keep liquid in stoppered bottle for a few weeks. Dilute with 4 parts of water to 1 of nicotine mixture. Spray on to roses. *Warning: This is poisonous – keep away from the fruit and vegetables.* (When you see what the nicotine does to the caterpillars, you may stop smoking.) *Keep away from children.*

597 Compost (1)
Only by feeding the soil can it be kept fertile. But don't buy peat for this purpose – make your own compost. What can you use? Grass cuttings, hedge clippings, fallen leaves, pea and bean stems, old spring and summer bedding plants; in fact, any soft green material that will rot easily. Some kitchen waste, like potato peelings, is also suitable. To hasten decomposition, a compost

accelerator needs to be scattered after every 6″ of compost.

598 Compost (2)
Many greengrocers have a problem: how to get rid of all the limp lettuces, collapsed cabbage leaves and festering fruit littering their floors. Some pay the local council to take it all away. Many would be grateful to you for removing it for free. It makes excellent compost.

599 Compost accelerator
Instead of layering with a branded compost-maker, simply add salt, soda and lime at intervals with the occasional bucket of water to hasten decomposition.

600 Creosote substitute
Next time you do an oil change, don't dispose of the dirty engine oil. Apply it to your garden fencing with an old brush — it's just as good as creosote for protecting the wood against insects and weather.

601 Earwig trap
Earwigs are especially fond of dahlias, so, if you have dahlias (or if you just don't like earwigs), you can make an earwig trap. This can be done by filling a flower pot with straw or hay and placing it upside down on a plant stake.

602 Fertilizers for roses
Roses like chopped banana skins to be dug in near their beds. They also have a taste for cold, weak tea and coffee dregs. (Funny things, roses!)

603 Fruit tree and rose bush fetilizer
The roots of fruit trees and rose bushes respond well to soap suds.

604 Garden broom
No need to buy a garden broom if you know how to make a really first-class one for nothing. First cut your twigs — birch or broom are the best — 1′ 6″ to 2′ in length. Make them into a bundle about 6″ in diameter at the top, untied. Now gather the twigs around a small stick (shorter and thinner than the one which you intend to use as the handle) and tie, first lightly, with string, and then, more firmly, with wire. Twist the wire ends together, using pliers. The stick for the handle should be about 3′

ᴵong, 1″ in diameter and sharpened at one end. The small stick is now pulled out and replaced by the handle, which is driven into position, point first.

605 Garden string
When nylon stockings are cut into 1″-wide strips, they curl inwards, on to themselves, to make a very strong 'string'. These short lengths can be tied together to form a long piece, which will be especially useful for staking trees and shrubs. The neutral colour blends very well into a garden background.

606 Garden tool rust preventative
Next time you drain the oil from your car sump, pour it into a large bucket of sand. Metal garden tools kept in this over the winter will not go rusty.

607 Hanging baskets
You can make very satisfactory hanging baskets for strawberries and other plants from half-gallon plastic containers. Enlarge the hole at the top (if the container has a top) to make room for the roots and make a drainage hole in the base. Suspend by handle.

608 Insecticide (1)
Rhubarb leaves are highly poisonous and can be made into an effective insecticide. Cut up 4 lb of rhubarb leaves and boil in 1 gallon of water for $\frac{1}{2}$ hour. Strain off the leaves and let the liquid cool. Store in ridged bottles, clearly marked 'Poison' and well out of reach of children. Before use, dissolve 4 oz of soft soap in 4 pints of hot water. When the water has cooled, add about 1 pint of rhubarb solution. Spray to destroy greenfly and blackfly. *This liquid is highly poisonous – do not spray on fruit or veg. Keep away from children.*

609 Insecticide (2)
Dissolve 1 oz soft soap in 1 pint water. Boil. Add 2 pints paraffin oil and agitate until thoroughly mixed. Use diluted – 1 part mixture to 10 parts water for hard-backs and 1 to 20 for soft insects. Apply by spray.

610 Liquid fertilizer
Take one dozen egg-shells. Place in 1 gallon of rainwater and soak for a month. (Keep yourself well to windward – it gives off a dark brown stench that could lift you out of your shoes. But your plants will appreciate it!)

611 Millipede and wireworm trap
Take a tall tin can and punch holes in it. Fill with vegetable and fruit peelings. Plant it upright in flower border with wire handle sticking out to mark the spot. Millipedes and wireworms are not very bright and will move in as squatters. Lift the can out of the ground once a week and burn contents.

612 Peas and beans
To get a good crop inexpensively, soak old newspapers in water for several hours, place along the bottom of the trench, cover with a thin layer of soil, then place the pea or bean seeds in position before finally topping with more earth.

613 Seeds (1)
Save the garden seeds which Nature hands out each year; dry, packet and label them – and plant next year.

614 Seeds (2)
Did you know that it is now possible to buy garden seeds which have been hermetically sealed in foil to preserve their germination and vitality for at least three years? It is likely that seeds will have more than doubled in price three years from now, so seeds bought now for planting in three years' time should prove a good long-term investment, always assuming that they are stored correctly. They are available from garden centres and some large stores.

615 Slug poison
Buy some fuel for portable irons, available from a hardware store. Mix with bran.

616 Slug and snail deterrent
Keep the dry ash from your garden fire, mix with a little soot and coal ash, and use it to dust seedlings and young vegetable crops to keep slugs and snails at bay. It also fertilizes the soil.

617 Vegetables – home-grown
So you have a large garden and plenty of ideas for growing vegetables, but no time to do the work. And, no doubt, within one mile from your home there are people with time to spare who love gardening – but have no garden. Why not put a small ad. in your local paper for someone willing to do the work and share the produce?

618 Vegetables – kitchen-grown
You can grow your own vegetables in the kitchen!
Lentils, mung beans, soy, millet, nuts, barley and other
grains can all be made to sprout with the aid of a seed
sprouter. The resulting crop of greens will be quick, fresh,
rather small, but very nutritious. They are excellent for
a salad. Fill one sixth of a pint jar with seeds. Cover with
water and allow to soak. Cap jar with piece of muslin and
secure with an elastic band. Morning and evening, rinse
seeds several times by pouring the water out of and into
the jar through the muslin. Finish by leaving the jar
empty of water and the seeds thoroughly washed. They will
start to sprout and be a couple of inches long and ready to
eat in about three days.

619 Weed or grass killer
For removing weeds or grass from parts of the garden
where they are not wanted (like between the cracks of
the crazy paving), household bleach does a very good job.

620 Weedkiller (1)
Before buying a branded weedkiller, try a kettle of boiling
water.

621 Weedkiller (2)
If boiling water (see no. 620) fails to shift the intruders,
try this: Half fill a bucket with water. Take from it about
1 pint and place in a smaller container. Add 1 oz copper
sulphate to the pint, mix thoroughly and pour back into
the bucket. Although not as deadly to human beings as
most of the branded weedkillers, this should be kept well
away from children, in a bottle marked: *'Poison! Do not
spray on fruit or veg.'*

How to save money on
Health
& Slimming

622   Anaemia – tonic
For anaemia, eat raw parsley. But don't overdo it – too much parsley can be bad for you.

623   Appetite stimulator
Two teaspoons of fresh tansy leaves (or 1 dried leaf) to 1 pint boiling water. Take 1 teacupful daily.

624   Bad breath treatment
1 oz of dried thyme leaves to 1 pint boiling water.

625   Barley water
Make your own lemon barley water from 2 tablespoons of pearl barley, ½ a lemon, sugar and 1 pint of water. Wash the barley thoroughly, place in a hot jug with the lemon juice, sliced rind and a little sugar. Cover with boiling water and leave to stand for 6 or 7 hours. Strain before use.

626   Black eyes and bruises
Apply crushed hyssop leaves to the bruise.

627   Blood purifier
Nettle tea made from 4 teaspoons of freshly chopped young nettle leaves to 1 teacup of boiling water and sweetened to taste. After pouring the boiling water on to the nettles, leave for 5 minutes and then strain.

628   Breath sweetener
After eating onions, garlic or drinking beer, an effective breath-deodorant is provided by chewing a sprig of parsley.

629 Bruises
Cover bruise immediately with a banana skin, soft side on to bruise. Bind into place with cold, wet bandages. This will reduce pain and minimise discolouration.

630 Catarrh treatment (1)
1 oz fresh young tops of hyssop to 1 pint boiling water. Infuse for 5 to 10 minutes. Drink frequently, instead of tea.

631 Catarrh treatment (2)
Relief from catarrh may be obtained by sniffing up the nose a few drops of mixture made from 1 teaspoon of common salt in a cup of warm water (soft water is better than hard). This should be done first thing in the morning and last thing at night. The mixture may be kept in a container and slightly re-warmed before use.

632 Flatulence relief
Two teaspoons powdered dill seeds to $\frac{1}{2}$ pint boiling water.

633 Foot care (1)
Hot feet in the summer? If you apply surgical spirit it will refresh and harden them.

634 Foot care (2)
A bowl full of warm water with a couple of tablespoons of vinegar added is a wonderful reviver of tired feet.

635 Gargle
Sore throat? There are few better gargles than a teaspoon of bicarbonate of soda plus a teaspoon of salt in a glass of warm water.

636 Gnat bite treatment
If applied at once, any of the following will give relief to an itching bite: raw onion, garlic pulp, cucumber juice, lemon juice or salt water.

637 Headache relief (1)
Try sage tea made from 3 teaspoons of freshly chopped sage and $\frac{1}{2}$ pint of boiling water. Pour the boiling water over the chopped sage, leave to infuse for 3-5 minutes, strain and sweeten to taste.

638 Headache relief (2)
A teaspoon of bicarbonate of soda mixed into the juice of a lemon is said to make an effective headache relief, without the aid of drugs.

639 Health salts
Make your own health salts. Ingredients: 2 oz of cream of tartar; 2 oz of tartaric acid; 2 oz bicarbonate of soda; 1 oz powdered magnesia; $\frac{1}{2}$ oz Epsom salts. Mix thoroughly.

Keep in a screw-top jar. Use by putting a teaspoonful in a glass of warm water.

640   Indigestion relief (1)
Chew a few coriander seeds just before eating. You can also make an infusion with 3 teaspoons dried coriander leaves or 1 teaspoon coriander seeds to 1 pint of boiling water.

641   Indigestion relief (2)
Mint leaves chewed raw are another good relief for indigestion. Or you could try mint tea.

642   Insect sting relief
Split open the stems of dandelions and apply the inner surface. Wasp stings respond well to either lemon juice or vinegar.

643   Insomnia treatment
Crumple a couple of bay leaves and place them under your pillow. Another remedy for sleeplessness is a cup of warm camomile tea drunk last thing at night.

644   Irritation soother
Instead of buying calomine lotion to soothe chicken pox or other types of spots, try a warm bath with 2 tablespoons of bicarbonate of soda.

645   Menstrual pain relief
Three teaspoons fresh leaves of lovage to 1 pint boiling water. Or, infuse 1 oz fresh young tops and leaves of rosemary with 1 pint of boiling water. Take teacupful daily.

646   Mouthwash
A cheap but refreshing mouthwash — a little lemon juice in water.

647   Nerve tonic
1 oz of fresh fennel leaves to 1 pint of boiling water makes a very soothing tonic.

648   Slimming aid (1)
A time-honoured (and inexpensive) method of slimming is to drink a pint of hot water 15 minutes before eating.

649   Slimming aid (2)
Place a handful of fennel leaves into 1 pint of water. Boil down to $\frac{1}{2}$ pint. Drink a wineglass of the liquid before meals.

650 Slimming exercise

Slimming diets can be expensive because all the high protein, low calorie foods are expensive. Therefore, you will save money if you can lose that spare tyre by doing a simple exercise which costs nothing. The following exercise is recommended because it is quick, easy – and highly effective. It enables many people to retain their normal waistline as well as their usual eating habits.

1 Stand upright with arms by the sides.

2 Breathe in deeply through the nose, filling the lungs so that the chest rises.

3 Breathe right out to empty the lungs completely.

4 Breathe in deeply, as before.

5 Breathe out once again, but, this time, as you exhale, bend forward slowly from the waist. Try to force out every last bit of air from lungs and stomach.

6 When all the air has gone, straighten gradually to an upright position *without breathing in*. (You will find that, because there is a partial vacuum in your tummy, air pressure outside the body presses the stomach inwards, making it far more concave than can be achieved in any other way.)

7 Remain in the upright position without breathing in for a few seconds. Then, inhale through the nose.

8 Repeat entire process.

If the exercise is performed every day before breakfast and after supper, an improvement in your waist measurement will soon result. Your stomach will draw in and flatten. In most instances, inches are taken off within only a few days.

651 Stye treatment

Bathe the eye with warm water during the day, and with salt and lukewarm water every morning and evening. (1 small teaspoon of salt to 1 pint of water.)

652 Sunburn treatment (1)

When you are really painfully sunburnt, the best cooling lotion there is (and the one used by hard-up Spaniards and Italians) is a half-and-half mixture of vinegar and cold water. Make a cupful. Soak a handkerchief in the lotion, squeeze it out and then lay it flat upon the affected area. You will see the steam rising and feel the heat dispersing. You will also smell like a salad, but it's a small price to pay for relief!

653 Sunburn treatment (2)

Make a paste of equal parts baking soda and water. Pat gently on to sunburnt area. Leave for half an hour. Wash off with cool water.

654 Teeth and gum treatment

Sage leaves rubbed over the teeth and gums not only clean them but also keep them strong and healthy.

655 Tonic

A wineglassful to a cupful of camomile tea drunk cold makes a good tonic. Place 1 oz of camomile flowers in 1 pint of boiling water and simmer for 15 minutes. Strain off the solids.

656 Vitamin C

Learn to recognise the rosehip in our hedgerows. It costs nothing and it is 20 times as rich in vitamin C as an orange. To make rosehip syrup, you need: 2 lb ripe rosehips; 1 lb sugar; $4\frac{1}{2}$ pints water. Mince the rosehips in a coarse mincer and place them into 3 pints of boiling water. Bring to the boil again. As soon as it reboils, remove the pan from the heat and leave for 15 minutes. Pour contents into a scalded jelly bag and allow most of the juice to drip through – do not squeeze. Return pulp to saucepan. Add $1\frac{1}{2}$ pints of water to pulp, reboil, allow to stand unheated for another 10 minutes. Drain as before. Pour juice into saucepan. Boil it down to about $1\frac{1}{2}$ pints, add sugar and boil for further 5 minutes.

How to save money on
Household Materials

657 Aerosols

Beware the aerosol can – it can more than double the cost of the product! An aerosol works by mixing a gas propellant with the product when sprayed from the tin. This has the effect of making the application quick and easy – but it also means that often you are paying more for the can and the gas than you are for the product. It is true, however, that some products go much further when mixed with a gas in this way. Shaving foam and sun cream are good examples of products which last for months because they have been mixed with gas. But there are many other substances which should be bought in ordinary containers, if your main concern is economy.

658 Alarm clock

If your alarm clock is growing old and feeble and no longer wakens you, don't buy a new one or order a telephone alarm call. Each night place the clock in a biscuit tin with a spoon in it and you will not oversleep.

659 Aluminium pan cleaner

Apple peelings provide one of the best ways of cleaning discoloured aluminium pans. Put the peel into the pan with water, bring to the boil and simmer for a few minutes.

660 Bath and sink cleaner – white enamel

Mix equal parts of linseed oil and real (not substitute) turpentine. Keep in a screw-top bottle. Do not use on stainless steel.

661 Batteries

If you have a home battery recharger, you can use it to revive run-down batteries for radios and toys at least once. Line up five or six batteries and tape them together.

Tape one terminal clip to each end. Give them about a minute – *no more, because if they are left too long they may explode.* Smaller, slimmer batteries, like those for some torches, will not take this treatment.

662 Beds

Good advice can save you money when purchasing a bed, mattress, divan or pillows and such advice is available from: *The National Bedding Federation Ltd., 251 Brompton Road, London SW3 2E2.* Please send a postage stamp when writing for information.

663 Bed sheets – new uses for old

Now that continental quilts are becoming more and more popular, the question is: What to do with the old bed sheets? Well, you will need the good ones as flat sheets for beneath the duvet. The thin or torn ones can sometimes be cut down to fit a child's bed. Or they can be converted into cot or pram sheets. Smaller pieces can make excellent tea-towels. Long strips, boiled, rolled and stored in plastic bags, can stand by as emergency bandages.

664 Blankets (1)

When a blanket wears thin in the middle, cut out a strip down the centre, including the worn part. Join together the outer edges so that they now form the centre strip of the new blanket. If possible, use a swing-needle sewing machine that does a 'stepped' blanket stitch, as this makes a flat joint. Hem the newly formed outer edges. Use the now smaller sheet either for a child's cot or bed or as a foot or shoulder blanket on an adult's bed.

665 Blankets (2)

If the side-to-middle operation described above is not possible, make pillowslips instead. Or make a supply of cot and pram sheets.

666 Brass and copper cleaner (1)

Take equal amounts of flour and salt and mix into a thick paste by stirring in a little vinegar. Plaster on to the metal and let it dry. Rinse and wipe.

667 Brass and copper cleaner (2)

Another way of cleaning brass or copper is to scrub it with a brush that has been dipped in ammonia. Rinse thoroughly in cold water. Dry. Polish.

For information about the collection and care of brass

and copper, contact *Brass and Copper Information Bureau, 109–110 Balsover Street, London W1P 7HF* (01–636 8862).

668 Brass cleaner
Salt mixed with lemon juice is another good brass cleaner. Or try a slice of lemon dipped in salt.

669 Candles
Hardly a year goes by that we do not need, for one reason or another, to buy in a large number of candles. They are not cheap, so why not make your own? The basics are wicks, waxes, stearic acid, hardener and, if you want coloured candles, dyes. All are available from: *Candlemakers Supplies, 4 Beaconsfield Terrace Road, London W14.*

670 Candles and tapers
You can get longer life out of your candles and tapers if you chill them in a refrigerator for about 24 hours before use.

671 Carpet colour freshener (1)
Mix one part vinegar to three parts boiling water. This mixture will freshen up the colours in your carpet. Simply dip a cloth into the solution, wring out well and wipe over gently. The slight smell of vinegar quickly disperses.

672 Carpet colour freshener (2)
Make a solution of ammonia – just a dash in warm water. Rub carpet with clean cloth dipped in the solution and wrung out.

673 Carpets
If you have a complaint about a woven carpet (Axminster or Wilton type), take it first to the retailer who sold you the carpet. If that fails, complain to the manufacturer. And if that fails, write to *The Federation of British Carpet Manufacturers, British Carpet Centre, Dorland House, 14–16 Lower Regent Street, London W1.*

674 Carpet shampoo (1)
Instead of buying a carpet shampoo, boil 1 lb of mild green washing soap in 1 gallon water. Add 1 oz of salts of tartar. Brush on to the carpet with a clean brush and rinse thoroughly with clean water.

675 Carpet shampoo (2)
Use warm water and a synthetic detergent of the kind recommended for washing wool or silk.

676 Chamois-leather polisher
These days, chamois-leather is quite expensive, so buy quite a small piece and stitch it to the centre of a large, soft duster. The chamois will form the polishing area in the middle when you grasp the duster sides.

677 Chewing gum stain removal
The best way of removing chewing gum from clothing is by attacking it with carbon-tetrachloride. If that fails, try freezing it off with a succession of small ice cubes – or one large piece of ice. The gum eventually turns brittle and may be crumbled away.

678 Chrome cleaner (1)
There is no better way of polishing chrome than by rubbing it with a dry cloth that has been dabbed into dry bicarbonate of soda.

679 Chrome cleaner (2)
Chrome can also be polished with a soft cloth dipped in ammonia.

680 Cleaner – all purpose
You know how a tablet of toilet soap can become soft, slimy and generally objectionable if it has been left too long in the bath water? You may be tempted to throw it away. Don't! Instead, put it into an aluminium pudding basin and pour boiling water on to it. This will produce a soapy jelly. When it has cooled, divide equally and place in large jam jars. To some of these add a little washing soda – and you will have an excellent floor, lino and woodwork cleaner. The remaining soapy jelly (with no washing soda) can be used for cleaning dishes, windows, lingerie, cars or work surfaces in the kitchen. If you have to wash something really filthy – something too greasy or sticky for even your washing soda jell (e.g. the inside of the oven) – add a little ammonia to the soapy jelly.

681 Cleaning clothes/hair brushes
You may have noticed that washing the bristles of a clothes or hair brush can shorten its life by ruining the wooden back of the brush. You can prevent this by rubbing the back with petroleum jelly before washing.

682 Cleaning glass bottles

Perfectly good and useful glass bottles are often thrown away because their owners can find no way of cleaning the stained inner surfaces. There is no need for this. Many stains will disappear after a mixture of vinegar and water has been shaken about in the bottle. If this fails, a strong solution of washing soda, warm water and a little lime will almost certainly succeed.

683 Cleaning kitchen tiles and sinks

Scouring powders are not necessary for the cleaning of kitchen tiles and sinks. A few drops of ammonia in warm water is just as effective.

684 Cleaning paintwork

Watered down washing-up liquid is perfectly good enough for cleaning paintwork if you do not have any of the all-purpose cleaner described in no. 680.

685 Cleaning saucepans and casseroles

No need to buy scouring powders to clean saucepans and casseroles. Household salt does this job very well.

686 Detergent (1)

Soaking whites overnight is still worth doing. It releases the dirt and means that you use less detergent.

687 Detergent (2)

Another way to substantially reduce the amount of washing powder needed by your washing machine is to add two or three tablespoons of sodium sesquicarbonate laundry water softener (obtainable from Boots). A 7-lb bag costs very little. And using it could save you about a cupful of washing powder for each wash. (You will need to experiment a little because the amount of saving will depend upon the hardness or softness of the water in your area.)

688 Detergent (3)

Rinse out an empty detergent packet with warm water for a suds bonus.

689 Detergent (4)

Next time somebody has a cold and you need to wash a pile of badly soiled handkerchiefs, resist the temptation to smother them in expensive biological detergent. Instead, soak in water with plenty of salt in it. Then wash normally.

690   Detergent (5)
If you live in the country, learn to recognise soapwort. There's plenty of it and, when boiled in water, it makes an effective detergent.

691   Dishcloth
Never throw away old string; it has many uses. One of them: string may be knitted or crocheted into a most effective dishcloth.

692   Dishwashers
Dishwashers are not yet common in this country, so, if you are buying one, it is likely to be your first. Therefore, it would be wise to consult the *Dishwasher Development Council, 25 North Row, London W1R 1DJ,* before spending your money.

693   Disinfectant
Disinfectant is expensive. In the summer, sprinkle the dustbin with borax, instead.

694   Distilled water
Did you know that the water which results from defrosting the fridge is *distilled* water? Don't pour it away; it can be used for car batteries and steam irons.

695   Dog chain
Before taking your dog for his holidays at the seaside, be sure to dip his chain (or metal parts of his lead) in clear varnish. If you don't do this, you will probably need to buy a new one at the end of the holiday because the sea air and water will turn it black with rust.

696   Dry cleaning (1)
Items of clothing which need dry cleaning, but do not need pressing, can be cleaned cheaply in the coin-operated machine at your local launderette.

697   Dry cleaning (2)
Save the cost of dry cleaning by sponging clothes lightly with a mixture of warm water and *Stergene,* using only the lather and being careful not to get the clothes too wet.

698   Dry cleaning fluid
For a do-it-yourself spot remover (for clothing) buy neat carbon-tetrachloride from the chemist.

699 Dustbin disinfectant
Soak a sheet of newspaper in the cheapest of disinfectants and tape it to the underside of the dustbin lid. It will keep away the flies far more cheaply than any of those blocks or powders. (Renew every week in the summer.)

700 Dyeing
You can avoid dyeing disasters by obtaining advice on any aspect of dyeing clothes, tie dyeing, fabric printing or painting. Write to the *Consumer Advice Bureau, Dylon International Ltd., Worsley Bridge Road, Lower Sydenham, London SE26 SHD.*

701 Envelopes (1)
By using sticky tape to reseal (and recycle) used envelopes, you can save pennies while also feeling self-righteous about the conservation of trees.

702 Envelopes (2)
Another way to save the cost of an envelope is to write a letter on one side of the paper only, then fold the paper into three (two folds) and seal the three open sides with sticky tape (preferably paper tape, which is the cheapest kind). Address the outside and stamp as with a normal envelope.

703 Fabrics
For information about British man-made fibres, you should write first to the manufacturer of the fabric. They usually supply very full details. However, if they cannot help, write to the following address, enclosing a large, stamped addressed envelope: *British Man-made Fibres Federation, Information Dept., Bridgewater House, 58 Whitworth Street, Manchester M14 DS.*

704 Fabric softener
Clean rainwater used for the final rinse will make fabrics beautifully soft.

705 Finger shields
Fingers cut from old rubber or plastic gloves make good finger shields to use when peeling vegetables.

706 Fire-lighter
If you need to light fires of solid fuel, save your old orange, lemon and potato peel until it has gone dry – it makes a most efficient fire-lighter.

707 Foil cups
Pies and frozen foods are often packed in little foil trays and cups which may be washed and used for a variety of jobs. They are useful in the fridge and freezer, for baking or for heating small quantities of food in the oven.

708 Freezers (1)
Before purchasing a freezer in order to buy meat in bulk, ask yourself whether you will, in fact, make use of all the various cuts obtained when you buy a fore-quarter of beef or a whole lamb. If your family won't eat fatty roasts (like stuffed breast of lamb) or stews, you cannot make the best use of a freezer because you are forced to buy selected cuts.

709 Freezers (2)
Large freezers are proportionately more economical than small ones in two ways. The first you can check for yourself by looking at prices of various models and dividing each price by the number of cubic feet for that freezer. And as models of more than 12 cubic feet carry no purchase tax, they are cheaper still. Most freezer owners are surprised by their own usage and wish that they had bought a larger model. Secondly, it is easier to recover operating costs on a big machine. For example, with a four-cubic foot freezer, you need to save 4p on the purchase price of every 1 lb of food to cover the cost of electricity. But with a 12-cubic foot model you would need to save only 2½p per pound to break even. The way to decide upon the *minimum* size for your family is to allow two cubic feet for each member of the family and add two extra. Thus, a family of four should have a model of at least ten cubic feet.

710 Freezers (3)
When buying a new freezer, be sure that it *is* a freezer and not a conservator. These will only keep previously frozen foods in a frozen state; they will not freeze food from room temperature. Be careful! Many people have already made this mistake. The appliance will freeze meat at home only if it has a fast freeze switch.

711 Freezers (4)
When buying, you will have to choose between a chest and an upright. Chests are both cheaper and more economical to run.

712 Freezers (5)
To use your freezer space economically, you must have some idea of how much space is needed for a given weight of meat. Remember, when meat is on the bone, you should allow two cubic feet (56½ litres) of space for every 25 lb of meat and bones; when meat has been boned, allow one cubic foot (28 litres) of space to 20 lb of meat.

713 Freezer bag-seals
Don't buy those paper-covered wire twisters for sealing freezer bags unless you're wealthy. Instead, go to your garden shop and buy a packet of 100 plastic-coated plant ties for only a few pence. Cut them in two — and you'll have 200! Or, if you don't mind fiddling, use string, which is cheaper still.

714 Freezer boxes
There is no holy writ which decrees that freezer boxes must be made of plastic. Cardboard boxes from the supermarket, so long as they are clean, make excellent freezer containers. Remove the flaps. Tie a length of strong string around the box so that it passes underneath (to give extra support) and across the open top (to form a handle).

715 Freezer boxes – plastic
Plastic freezer boxes are ideal for storing soft fruit in the freezer because, unlike foil containers, they will not react with the acid in the fruit. But these are relatively expensive. If you try to use the cheaper plastic freezer bags, however, the fruit will squash together and freeze into a solid mass. The way around this problem is to spread the washed and drained fruit on a baking tray and place in the freezer. When frozen hard, place the fruit in plastic freezer bags and return to the freezer.

716 Freezer food containers
Plastic margarine or yoghurt tubs are excellent for storing goods in the freezer.

717 Freezer insurance (1)
If you have a freezer cabinet crammed with food, it might be a sensible precaution to spend about £4 on insurance to cover £100 worth of perishables being ruined by power cut or electrical fault. This could be part of a home contents policy.

718 Freezer insurance (2)

There is one kind of risk against which no insurance company will insure – the loss of food caused by accidentally switching off the freezer. This could happen all too easily if left to chance. Three precautions that you could take are: (a) make use of (or have installed) an entirely independent socket for the freezer, so that it is in no way connected to any other electrical apparatus; (b) have the freezer fitted with a red neon indicator light which glows continuously while the machine is switched on; (c) tape down the freezer switch so that it is permanently on.

719 Furniture scratch remover

Pour cod liver oil on to scratched polished furniture and leave. Then polish.

720 Glass cleaners

Methylated spirits is a cheap and effective window and mirror cleaner. Cheaper still is vinegar and hot water. And even cheaper – tea strained from the pot.

For information about choosing and looking after all kinds of domestic glassware (except flat, plate glass), send a large, stamped addressed envelope to the *Glass Manufacturers' Federation, 19 Portland Place, London W1N 4BH.* For flat glass (including that used for double glazing), write to: *The Glass Advisory Council, 6 Mount Row, London W1.*

721 Greaseproof paper

No need to buy greaseproof paper for lining cake tins. Just remove the greaseproof inner bags from your cereal packets.

722 Grease stain removal

Spots of grease may be removed from upholstery by rubbing corn meal into them, leaving them for several hours and then vacuum cleaning, brushing, and vacuum cleaning again.

723 Greasing cake tins

Save butter and/or margarine wrappers for greasing cake tins.

724 Handkerchiefs

Cotton handkerchiefs can be used and washed and used

indefinitely and are, therefore, much cheaper than disposable paper tissues.

725 Home
The Building Centre is a mine of information about almost everything to do with the home. Whether your problem be central heating, double glazing, window frames, floor or wall coverings, ironmongery, bathroom fittings and accessories, or kitchen units and equipment, you need only telephone the Building Centre for advice, or for the name of the most suitable manufacturers to contact. If you are in London, a visit to the permanent exhibition at the Building Centre is well worth while. *The Building Centre, 26 Store Street, London WC1E 7BT (01–637 4522).*

726 Home washing
Today, clothing is made from so many different fabrics that one has to be careful when washing them. Errors can be costly. Of course, you should always follow the instructions provided with the garment, but sometimes one loses them. Inspect the garment to see whether it has attached to it one of the Home Laundering Consultative Council labels. The HLCC has formulated eight processes for the machine washing of different fabrics. These are listed on the sides of packets of washing powder. If still in doubt, contact the *HLCC, 41/42 Dover Street, London W1X 4DS (01–493 7446).*

727 Hot water-bottle preservative
The first time you use a new hot water-bottle, put a little glycerine in just before filling it with water. This will protect the rubber and extend its life.

728 Household bleach
Instead of buying branded household bleach, why not do what great-grandmother did and make your own? Dissolve 1 lb of washing soda in two pints of boiling water. Mix $\frac{1}{2}$ lb of chloride of lime with four pints of cold water and allow to settle. Strain off the clear liquid and pour it into the dissolved washing soda. Again, allow to settle and strain off the clear liquid. Store this in dark bottles, preferably in a dark place, and label clearly. This is an excellent bleach for white cottons or linens, but should not be used on other fabrics. Use with an equal amount of hot water. When stains have been removed, do *not*

allow the bleach to dry into the fabric. Wash it out very thoroughly in cold water.

729 Household powder cleaners
Most packets of scouring/floor cleaning/washing powder have either perforated corners bearing the words 'Press here, then tear back' or a number of large perforated circles which the manufacturers suggest you should 'Press out to pour'. Instead of doing anything so rash, pierce one small hole with a screwdriver. Your powder will last much longer.

730 Ironing board cover
Old pyjama trousers may be slipped over your ironing board to form a new cover.

731 Jewellery cleaning
If you periodically take jewellery into a jeweller to be cleaned, you can save money by doing the job yourself, although probably you will not do it quite so well as the craftsman. Assuming that the items are precious jewellery set firmly in metal, proceed as follows: Make a lather from toilet soap and warm water. Dip in the piece of jewellery and scrub gently but persistently with an old, soft toothbrush. Dry with a linen glass cloth or old linen handkerchief. Rub lightly with a soft, clean leather to give the final sparkle. Some of the more expensive costume jewellery, which is also metal-set, may be cleaned in the same way. Do not wash costume jewellery when the stones have been cemented into place.

732 Kettle defurring
Remove lid, turn upside down and shake out loose fur. Put two teaspoons of borax into the kettle and fill with water. Bring to boil. Wash away the softened deposit. Repeat until clean.

Never leave a kettle with hot water cooling in it; it is depositing fur all the time.

733 Kitchen foil
Kitchen foil can be re-used again and again if it is carefully washed, smoothed flat and stored in a special place of its own.

734 Kitchen jars
Large, screw-top instant coffee jars can be made to look

attractive and expensive with the aid of either a little enamel paint or adhesive-backed plastics. Choose your colours to match the kitchen colour scheme.

735 Kitchen paper rolls (1)
Disposable paper towels in the kitchen are strictly for people with disposable paper money. Use terrycloth hand towels every time.

736 Kitchen paper rolls (2)
If you *must* use paper rolls for the kitchen, buy the softer two-ply rolls which are just as efficient but much cheaper.

737 Knitting wool
If you are knitting a girl's jumper which will *always* be worn under a pinafore dress, you need only buy the wool for the parts of the jumper which will show. The parts which will be hidden under the pinafore may be knitted from spare wool, providing it is of the same thickness.

738 Laundering (1)
If you have a guest room, save cleaning bills by keeping the bedspread inside-out until the day your guests arrive.

739 Laundering (2)
You can also reduce laundry bills by 'topping and tailing' your bed sheets. The upper half of the bottom sheet always gets more wear — and looks more soiled — than the lower half. So, instead of getting the sheet washed when the top half looks ready for it, swing it round so that the still unsullied half is now at the top. When that begins to look dingy, turn the sheet over and start again.

740 Leather (1)
If you have anything made of leather — chairs or settees or even leatherbound books — in a room which is centrally heated, do not forget that the leather will need regular nourishment from either furniture or shoe polish.

For information about leather in all its forms and how to care for it, write to: *The Leather Institute, Leather Trade House, 9 St. Thomas Street, London SE1 9SA.*

741 Library fines
Library charges are now such that, if your book is long overdue, it can prove quite expensive. Do not forget that it is possible to renew books by telephone. This is

especially worth doing when you have several library books. (Always telephone after 1.00 pm when calls are on a cheaper rate.)

742 Light bulbs
Single coil light bulbs last just as long as coiled coil filament bulbs, but cost 5 or 6p less. However, coiled coil bulbs do give about 14% more light.

743 Mahogany – mark remover
Marks on mahogany furniture caused by heat or damp can be inexpensively removed by gently rubbing in a little metal polish on a soft, dry cloth.

744 Metal cleaner
Toothpaste is cheaper than metal polish and it will clean any kind of metal, although a little more 'elbow grease' is necessary. Apply with an old toothbrush.

745 Metal cleaners and polishers
Some of these are sold in metal bottles with narrow necks. Therefore, the only way to get at the last drop is by removing the bottom with a tin-opener.

746 Metal scrap
Never throw away old metal – it's like throwing away money. Aluminium, lead, copper and brass all fetch good prices from local scrap metal merchants, whose names you can find in the Yellow Pages. Check them before you start to collect. You can also send aluminium to *International Alloys Ltd., Bicester Road, Aylesbury,* who will pay several p. per lb and provide sacks, if requested. Metal caps and pull tabs from soft drinks and beer cans will also earn you money. Contact International Alloys for their current prices and work out what sort of profit you can make, bearing in mind carriage charges.

747 Oven cleaner (1)
If your desire to clean the inside of the cooker *cheaply* is greater than your wish to clean the inside of the cooker *easily*, the following method costs less than any of the branded aerosol products. First, mix one tablespoon of flour with a little water to make a thin cream. Now, dissolve one tablespoon of caustic soda in half pint boiling water. Add the cream to the boiling water and mix thoroughly. Apply to the inside of the cooker with a mop and brush. If you have more than you need, you can

bottle and store it. But if you do, be sure to use a ridged poison bottle, clearly labelled and kept on a high shelf.

748 Oven cleaner (2)

Another way of cleaning the inside of the oven is by mixing a tablespoon of ammonia into two pints of hot water. Slosh the mixture about on the inside of the oven, particularly on the greasy parts, and leave overnight. You will find that, in the morning, a wet rag will wipe the oven clean with very little effort (or expense).

749 Oven cleaner (3)

Yet another way of cleaning a greasy oven is by placing an open dish of ammonia containing a rag inside the oven and leaving it there overnight. Next day, remove the ammonia and wash the oven either with hot water containing a detergent or, better, with the washing soda jell described in no. 680.

750 Oven cleaner (4)

Ordinary ovens can be virtually converted into the non-stick type by the following treatment: Mix a tablespoon of bicarbonate of soda with half a pint of water and wipe all over the inside of the oven – door, roof, wire racks, every-thing. Leave. After every usage, wipe with a damp cloth and repeat the treatment. You will find that stains will gradually disappear until your oven becomes a thing of beauty.

751 Packaging for the post

Never throw away the cardboard tubes which cooking foil comes wrapped around – they are just right for sending papers through the post. But don't forget to tape up the ends !

752 Plastic bowls

If you take an empty half-gallon plastic orange juice container and carefully saw off its base, using a fine-tooth saw, you have made yourself a very fair cereal or soup bowl.

753 Plastics

The British Plastics Federation will advise enquirers where they may obtain specific materials, products, machinery and services and also identify trade names. *British Plastics Federation, 47 Piccadilly, London W1V 0DN (01–734 2041).*

754 Polishers/dishcloths

Everyone should keep a rag bag for old underclothing, sheets and soft cloths. Old socks, folded inside and sewn (each to form a pad) are excellent as polishers. Cellular underwear makes very good dishcloths.

755 Polish – floor

Wax floor polish can be eked out if a little white spirit (or turpentine substitute) is added. The polish goes on more easily, too.

756 Polishers – furniture

Tissue paper makes an excellent polisher for waxed furniture. Therefore, never throw any away ; when it arrives as packing, gift wrapping paper or in laundry boxes, fold it up and store with your polish.

757 Polish – furniture (1)

If you *must* disguise the beauty of wood grain by covering it with furniture polish, at least you may save on the cost of the polish by making your own. Buy a pint of turpentine and one quart of boiled linseed oil. Mix. Another method is to grate 1 oz of beeswax into a jam jar and fill to the top with (real) turpentine. Leave for a few days until wax is fully dissolved. Stir.

758 Polish – furniture (2)

Make a mixture of two parts paraffin oil to one part vinegar. Soak some clean rags (natural fibres, like cotton, are the best) in the mixture. Keep adding rags until all the mixture has been absorbed. Leave for about 30 minutes. Ring out. Dry. You now have a supply of impregnated polishers which will do a first-class job on furniture, windows and mirrors.

759 Polish – tile

There is no better way of getting a high polish on ceramic or mosaic tiles than by rubbing with old newspaper.

760 Polish – wood and glass

Cold tea from the pot is good for cleaning mahogany, varnished woodwork or polished mirrors.

761 Postage

You can cut down the weight of a parcel and, conse-quently, the postage charges by using old polystyrene ceiling tiles instead of cardboard when packing something fragile. Cut it to size and then wrap with brown paper.

762 Post Office – complaints

If you have a specific complaint to make to the Post Office (not a general grumble about telephone or postal charges), contact the manager of your local Office. If that doesn't bring satisfaction, try the *Post Office Users' National Council (POUNC), Waterloo Bridge House, Waterloo Road, London SE1*, or the *Telephone Users' Association, 35 Connaught Square, London W2*. (The latter charges a membership fee.)

763 Pottery

If you fit the taps over your kitchen sink with rubber nozzles, you will reduce the number of broken cups, saucers and plates.

To find the manufacturers and stockists of different kinds of pottery, or for any information regarding pottery or china, contact. *British Ceramic Manufacturers' Federation, Federation House, Stoke-on-Trent ST4 2SA (0782 48631)*.

764 Puppy/baby stain remover

If you have a puppy/baby that leaves puddles on carpets, it is wise to have a bottle of stain remover at the ready. Make this by mixing $\frac{1}{2}$ cup white vinegar with $1\frac{1}{2}$ cups warm water. Mop up worst of puddle, then apply mixture.

765 Quilt

If you make your own bed quilt, you can save around £100 by today's prices. Cut an old sheet into 18″ squares. On to the centre of each of these sew patterns cut from old shirts, pyjamas and dresses. Join the squares, edge to edge, to make up the required size. For a couple of pounds you can buy quilt lining material for the underside, or you can use an old blanket. Cut the underside to the same area as the (squared) topside. Machine the two together at 18″ intervals, along the side of the squares.

766 Razor blades

If you use a wet shave razor with blade, keep its head (including blade) inside a tumbler half filled with surgical spirit. This will prolong the life of the blade.

767 Rubber bands

Old rubber gloves make excellent rubber bands if they are cut into $\frac{1}{2}$″ or 1″ widths.

768 Scorched pan cleaner

If a pan is scorched really badly, pour into it a couple of inches of water and add a tablespoon of washing soda. Put this on the stove and boil vigorously.

769 Scorch mark remover

You can remove ironing scorch marks by soaking the article in a solution of one part glycerine to two parts water. Then wash normally.

770 Scouring pads – plastic

Easily cleaned scourers for dishes, pans and work tops may be made from the plastic net-bags in which supermarkets pack some of their fruit and vegetables.

771 Scouring pads – steel wool (1)

Do not throw away tinfoil after using it for cooking. Instead, wash and dry it. Roll into a firm ball and use in place of a steel wool scouring pad. It will remove stains efficiently from pans and dishes.

772 Scouring pads – steel wool (2)

Those soapy scouring pads of wire wool are usually larger than needed for the job and, once wet, they tend to rust rapidly. You can avoid the first problem by cutting the pads in half. You can delay the second by drying the pads in the oven (but only do this in the cooling off period after the oven has been used for cooking).

773 Scouring pads – steel wool (3)

Steel wool cleaning pads often go rusty and become unusable because they are left in water. If you attach a plastic clothes peg to one (by a length of thread or string) and use it to hang the pad away from the water, it will last much longer.

774 Scouring powder

1 lb pumice powder (yes, you can get it from the very large chemists!) ; $\frac{3}{4}$ lb soap powder. Mix. Keep dry.

775 Sewing machine oil

Paraffin is very suitable for the purpose – but remember that it is highly inflammable.

776 Sewing needles

To sharpen old sewing needles, 'sew' a piece of fine emery paper through and through.

777 Shelf lining paper

Why use expensive shelf paper when you can cover your cupboard shelves with wallpaper (if you haven't any end-of-roll pieces, call at any wallpaper shop for cheap rolls of discontinued patterns). If you don't mind doing without the pattern, lining paper is cheaper still.

778 Shoe cleaning

If you have a few drops of lemon juice left over from cooking, don't waste it! Find a pair of shoes that need cleaning and use it to give them a shine.

779 Shoe polish

The last of the shoe polish always goes hard in the tin. Add half teaspoon of olive oil and mix into the polish to render it usable.

780 Shoe polish – for light-coloured leather

Ingredients: 8 oz turps; 8 oz warm water; 3 oz white wax; a little liquid ammonia. Melt wax. Add turpentine and water. Pour in ammonia until it thickens into a cream.

781 Shopping bag – plastic

You can repair a polythene shopping bag which has split at the seams by ironing. Place a layer of brown paper – or a couple of sheets of newspaper – on your ironing board, then the bag. Slip another sheet of paper inside the bag to prevent the plastic sticking to itself *except at the part you are mending*. Finally, lay yet another sheet of paper over the bag and iron on to that, never directly on to the plastic.

782 Silver cleaning

If you are one of those lucky people with a mass of silver to keep clean, rubbing away with toothpaste (see no. 744) would take too much time and energy. So, this is what to do: Pour a quart of water into a large aluminium saucepan. Add one tablespoon of salt and one tablespoon of bicarbonate of soda. Bring to the boil. Pop a few pieces of cutlery into the water and boil for three or four minutes. Pick them out with tongs and put in the next lot.

783 Silver polish

Mix $\frac{1}{4}$ lb of soap scraps (or soft soap) with $\frac{1}{4}$ lb whiting. Pour two and a half cups of boiling water over mixture and stir until completely melted. Put in a jar and use as a silver dip.

784 Sink cleaner
To clean that old porcelain sink, use a little of the household bleach described in no. 728.

785 Soap (1)
One way of using up the last scrap of toilet soap is to grate it and mix in with washing powder for use in the washing machine.

786 Soap (2)
Another way is to save several pieces and boil them up with water the next time there are 'smalls' – undies and handkerchiefs – to be washed.

787 Stain removal
Many stains on clothes which people send to the dry-cleaners could be removed at home, for nothing, without benefit of biological detergent. Try cold water first. Put an old cloth under the stained material and then pat the stain repeatedly with a cold, wet sponge. At the same time, move the material about so that there is always clean cloth immediately under the stain. Let it dry naturally.

788 Stain removal – blood
Wash at once or soak in cold salt solution (one level tablespoonful to one pint water).

789 Stain removal – fats of all kinds
These include oil, cream, ice cream, chocolate, lipstick. Scrape off any visible surface layer of fat very gently, so as not to damage the fabric. Either wash in hot, soapy water and rinse thoroughly or, if this is not practicable, use a solvent like carbon-tetrachloride.

790 Stain removal – fruit, beer, coffee and tea
Fruit, beer, coffee and tea stains are best removed by hot water. Stretch the material over a metal pudding basin, keeping the stain in the middle, and secure the material around the sides with string or a rubber band. Place the basin, stain uppermost, in the bottom of your bath or wash basin. You now need to climb on to a chair or stepladder so that you are a good distance above the stain, taking a kettle full of boiling water with you. Pour the water straight down on to the stain (taking care not to splash the cat or your ankles!). In this way, stains can be removed by a combination of heat and force of

water. If both cold and hot water fail to shift a stain, soak in borax solution (one level teaspoon borax to one gill warm water). But do not use borax for baby's nappies or underclothes. Always wash borax out of any garment very thoroughly. If this fails, a not-too-strong solution of household bleach (chlorine-type) will almost certainly succeed. But be careful with coloured materials, if possible testing the affect of the bleach on some tiny hidden area which will not show.

791 Stain removal – grass
Sponge with meths. Wash or sponge with a detergent.

792 Stain removal – ink
Many inks wash out easily, but some (including marking ink) are more stubborn. Try methylated spirits on a clean rag. If that doesn't work, sponge with a solution of salts of lemon or oxalic acid in water (one level teaspoon to half gill warm water).

793 Stain removal – lipstick
The worst of it may be removed by carbon-tetrachloride. Remaing traces can be eliminated by hydrogen peroxide – *but be careful: hydrogen peroxide may bleach the material.* The best plan is to use it beside the sink, with the cold water tap running. Apply a small amount for a few seconds, then rinse off.

794 Stain removal – mildew
Bleach according to the fabric, using a hypochlorite bleach (like *Domestos, Parazone,* or *Durazone*) for cottons and linens, and hydrogen peroxide for silks and woollens. Dilute the hypochlorite bleach according to the instructions on the bottle. Dilute hydrogen peroxide one part hp to two parts warm water.

795 Stain removal – milk
Ether will remove most of the stain. Use a strong solution of borax (1 tablespoon borax to $\frac{1}{4}$ pint water) to remove the rest. Then wash with clean water.

796 Stain removal – nail varnish
Start with acetone. Follow with methylated spirits. Wash.

797 Stain removal – paint
Sponge with neat turpentine or turps substitute. Then wash out or, if a small area, sponge thoroughly.

798 Stain removal – perspiration

Perspiration stains may be removed by soaking the garment for an hour in a solution of one handful of salt and a quart of water.

799 Stain removal – rust/iron mould

Rust stains can be removed from clothing by alternate applications of lemon juice and warm water. Alternatively, in sunny weather, apply the lemon juice and leave cotton or linen to bleach in the sun. If this fails, cover the mark with oxalic acid crystals and pour boiling water through them. Then allow to steep in the solution. Wash thoroughly afterwards.

800 Stain removal – tar

First loosen and soften by rubbing grease (butter will do) into the stain. Then remove as for fats (see no. 789).

801 Stain removal – wines and spirits

Fairly recent stains will respond to gentle sponging with warm water and detergent. Older ones are best removed by methylated spirits.

802 Starch

Cold water starch is cheaper than spray-on starch. Mix two tablespoons of powdered starch with two tablespoons of cold water into a smooth paste. Add a pint of cold water.

803 Sweeping brush

A new broom with natural (not plastic) bristles will last longer if you soak the bristles in cold salt water and allow to dry before using for the first time.

804 Tablecloth stain prevention

For avoiding stained tablecloths (and the cost of getting them clean again) there is one infallible method: don't use them. Wipe-over place mats, which allow you to see the beauty of a table's natural woodgrain, are much more sensible.

As for the table, avoid French polish like the plague. These days, there are numerous modern finishes which allow you to see the grain in the timber, do not react neurotically to heat (as does French polish), may be cleaned by wiping with a damp cloth, and which are quite inexpensive. Dare I suggest that a good woodgrain, very lightly stained to accentuate the wood's natural highlights and varnished with a clear, matt varnish (which is invisible, as well as heat and stain resistant), looks infinitely better than the table plastered with the shiniest, most expensive French polish? Incidentally, the matt varnish finish also saves a fortune in furniture polish.

805 Table-top stain remover

Dark table-tops have a nasty way of acquiring white circles, caused by hot cups and the like. What to do? First, try a mixture of cigarette ash and either olive oil or turpentine, gently rubbed into the spot with a circular movement of your rag. If that fails, try camphorated oil (and no cigarette ash). If *that* fails, you will have to admit defeat and spend some money upon a branded product. There are some excellent ones.

806 Telephone bills (1)

Local STD calls cost only one quarter of the standard rate before 8 am, after 6 pm, or at weekends. Local and trunk calls cost most between 9 am and 1 pm, Monday–Friday. Why not type or write out this information and stick it on your phone, below the dial?

807 Telephone bills (2)

Many households keep a money-box by the phone for people to make their payments on-the-spot. This has two advantages: firstly, it does reduce the length of conversations by making speakers more aware of the cost; secondly, when the phone bill arrives, it is very reassuring to be able to pay most of it straight from the box (although this is a matter of convenience, not economy). The system often breaks down because people do not happen to have the right change at the time. An easy way around this problem is to keep a jar of buttons, tiddly-winks or – if you are cultivating an upper middle class image – roulette counters, by the phone. When a call is made, people put either money or, if short of change, counters into the money-box. Each weekend there is a reckoning during which the counters are replaced by hard cash.

808 Telephone bills (3)

Never hang on for somebody who is not immediately available and do not volunteer to call again. Leave a message for the person to call you. Even if you do have to call him again, it is very likely that this will still be cheaper than hanging on. For trunk and overseas calls, it is usually worth asking the operator for a person-to-person call, especially to a crowded building like a factory or hotel.

809 Telephone bills (4)
Much expensive telephone time is wasted because the caller is not properly organised. Before making a call, jot down a list of brief headings covering all the points you wish to discuss. Doing this can easily halve the duration of the call because it eliminates thinking time. Make sure that everything you may need during the call – paper, pen, reference books, etc. – is to hand.

810 Telephone bills (5)
Before making a trunk or overseas call, always check the charge rate before dialling. There have been many occasions when telephone subscribers have run up enormous bills because they simply did not realise how much their calls were costing.

811 Towels (1)
When towels become worn to a hole, instead of discarding them, try darning the thin part with candlewick cotton. In this way you can prolong the life of a tatty towel indefinitely.

812 Towels (2)
When buying towels, remember that small ones – although cheaper in the short term – are not as economical as big ones in the long term. They get soaked too quickly, need more washing and wear out more rapidly.

813 Trouser shine remover
Add one tablespoon ammonia to one pint of hot water. Dip a clean, cotton ironing cloth into the solution and squeeze out. Press the cloth down on to the shiny garment using a medium warm iron.

814 Vacuum cleaners
If your shaggy dog leaves hairs all over the house, you probably spend a lot of time and electricity vacuuming them up. You could save most of this by vacuuming the dog, instead. He would enjoy it and the RSPCA have no objection.

815 Vases
When you get a fine crack in a vase, you can sometimes

seal this by painting a coat of clear varnish on the inside.

816 Wash basin cleaner

If you keep your toilet soap on a small pad of foam rubber, this may be used for cleaning the wash basin.

817 Water softener

A little borax in your washing up or bath water softens it effectively. And soft water saves soap (as well as electricity – see no. 532).

818 Wrapping sandwiches

These days we all wrap our sandwiches in expensive tinfoil or that clear, clingy cellophane. We could save this expense by using a coloured greaseproof bread wrapper.

How to save money on

Knowing Your Rights

819 Capital Transfer Tax
If a man leaves his entire estate to his widow there is no capital transfer tax.

820 Central heating
If you live in an area which is being made into a smokeless zone under the Clean Air Act, you may qualify for a grant towards the installation of central heating. Enquire at the local town hall.

821 Death grant
When a person who has made satisfactory National Insurance payments dies, a 'death grant' of £30 can be claimed by his/her family to help pay the funeral expenses. It must be claimed within six months of the death, however. Information from Social Security Office (Leaflet NI 49).

822 Debt recovery
If you're going to take legal action to recover a debt, you must do so within six years of the loan. After that time, your right to sue is lost, unless revived by any acknowledgement or part payment, in which case the six-year period starts over again. (But there are special exceptions in the cases of fraud, mistake or concealment.)

823 Dental treatment
Dental treatment is normally half price up to a maximum of £10. If you are on a low income and find the half price difficult to meet, apply for help from Social Security (by filling in Form F1D, which your dentist should be able to give you). Treatment is free to (a) all children under 16 and persons aged 16 and over at school full-time; (b) expectant mothers and mothers who have borne a child during the preceding 12 months.

824 Disabled person's help from local authority
Local authorities are willing to help handicapped people in all sorts of ways – for example, by paying their telephone rental charges. Sadly, many do not receive such help simply because the local authority does not know of them. Information from local Social Services Department. (Leaflet HB1 gives details of all help available to handicapped people.)

825 Disabled person's attendance allowance
A severely disabled person who needs considerable help and supervision from others may claim an attendance allowance. The amount varies according to whether attendance is needed for both day and night. Information from Social Security Office.

826 Divorced woman's child's special allowance
When a divorced woman's ex-husband dies (and he has been paying towards the upkeep of a child of the marriage), she is entitled to a child's special allowance *in addition to family allowance*. Information from Social Security Office.

827 Education – grants for talented children
If your child has special gifts – for example, musical or theatrical – you may obtain a grant from your local education authority to maintain the child at a special private school where those gifts may be developed. But the child will need to be obviously talented in order to get (a) a strong recommendation from his/her existing school, and (b) a favourable audition from the target school. Information from local Education Office.

828 Engagement ring
Legally, an engagement ring need not be returned to the man, even if the marriage does not take place, unless it is a family heirloom. Moral to young men: don't give an engagement ring unless (a) you are very sure that the marriage will take place or (b) it is a family heirloom.

829 Expectant mothers (1)
Expectant mothers can claim £25 'maternity grant' if either wife or husband is making National Insurance Contributions. Claim must be made from nine weeks before expected week of confinement to three months after the birth. Divorced women can claim on their ex-husband's

insurance, providing the divorce took place within nine weeks of the week in which the baby is expected, and that the claim is made before confinement. Single women can claim only on their own insurance. Information from Social Security Office or Child Health Clinic.

830   Expectant mothers (2)
Expectant mums who have been paying full rate National Insurance Contributions can also claim a 'maternity allowance' for about 18 weeks, starting in the eleventh week before the baby is expected and continuing until six weeks after the baby is born. Cash is not paid until she stops work, however, as the idea is to help working women to take time off to have their babies. In addition an earnings related supplement is paid for the whole period. These should be claimed between the fourteenth and eleventh week before the expected week of confinement. If claimed more than six weeks after the birth, however, it is likely that no payment will be made. Information from Social Security Office or Child Health Clinic.

831   Extra grant for blind people
There is no special pension, as such, for blind people. But if a blind person registers with the local Social Services Department, he or she may receive an extra £1.25 on top of the Supplementary Benefit. Also, the Social Services Department may have other welfare facilities available. Information from local Social Services Department.

832   Eye tests
Do not pay anything for an eye test – this is available free under the NHS. However, first you must get a note from your doctor.
Lenses cost up to £3.50. Try not to be tempted by the fancy frames offered by the opticians – they may cost over 30 times as much as the National Health ones, which are perfectly good and come in an extensive range, although opticians generally have only a handful on view. Your local Family Practitioner Committee should be able to show you all the frames available.

833   Family allowance
When the baby is the mother's second, family allowances become payable to the mother at the rate of £1.50 per week. Information from Social Security Office.

834 Free advice

Free expert advice is available on almost every subject – everything from family planning to how to get a divorce! The best place to start is the Citizen's Advice Bureau – or the Readers' Service Department of Mirror Group Newspapers (telephone: 01-267 4455).

835 Guardian's allowance

When both parents are deceased (at least one of them having made satisfactory National Insurance payments) the guardian of the child can claim a 'guardian's allowance' equal to the child's special allowance (see no. 848). It must be claimed within three months of the child concerned having been orphaned. Information from Social Security Office.

836 Having a baby

Can you afford to have a baby? Well, if you buy baby's things sensibly, you can get them (new) for about £160 – and the Welfare State will pay you £224.80 (18 weeks at £11.10 plus £25 maternity grant) plus – possibly – an 'earnings related supplement'.

So the answer is: yes, you can! Even so, before finally deciding to have a family, it is not a bad idea to try living for a month on the husband's salary alone. Besides teaching you a lot about the making of economies, this will also yield a small baby fund.

837 Health Service – prescription exemptions

You probably know that there is a charge of 20p on each NHS prescription. But did you know that this does not apply to children under 16, people over retirement age, expectant or nursing mothers, disablement pensioners, and people receiving supplementary allowances or family income supplement? Also, if you are on a low income, you can claim exemption or help by filling in Form PC11, obtainable from your local Post Office or Social Security Office.

838 Health Service – season ticket prescriptions

If you need very frequent prescriptions, you can save by buying a 'season ticket' or 'prepayment certificate'. (The present cost is £2 for six months, £3.50 for a year.) To obtain the certificate, complete and submit Form FP95/EC95, available from Post Offices, Social Security Offices and Family Practitioner Committees.

839   Home improvement or extension
If you borrow money from a building society or bank in order to improve your home, don't forget that you can get income tax relief on the interest. Relief is also available on interest paid on certain types of loans from finance companies.

840   House conversion into flats
When a large house is to be converted into flats, its owner may obtain a grant. Information from Council Offices.

841   House owners' home improvement grants
Do you own an 'older' house which you wish to improve, or convert into flats? Or does your house lack such basic amenities as a bathroom, hot and cold water or a lavatory? Or do you share with other households a house which lacks standard amenities? Or is your house badly in need of repair and situated in a housing action area or a general improvement area? If so, you *may* qualify for a home improvement, intermediate, special or repair grant. These grants (which provide a percentage – never the full amount – of the cost) cover a wide range of work needed to raise the standard of a house or to keep it in good repair. The applicant must be the freeholder or have a lease with at least five years to run. This includes both owner-occupiers and landlords. A person with a short tenancy cannot apply, but, if the landlord is unwilling to carry out improvements, the tenant can ask the local council to require him to install any of the missing standard amenities. Full details from Council Offices.

842   Income tax (1)
Are you paying too much income tax? It is estimated that about half of all wage and salary earners are, simply because they do not understand the tax system. Here are a few guidelines:
All tax calculations are made from 6th April to the following 5th April. What was the *gross* amount of all your taxable income between those dates? *Note:* you do *not* pay tax on: income from a scholarship; educational grants; the first £40 interest on National Savings Bank ordinary accounts; accrued interest on National Savings Certificates; Social Security benefits such as family income supplement, invalidity benefit, unemployment benefit, maternity benefit, sickness benefit; regular gifts of

money of £1,000 or less received (unless paid under a legally binding obligation). Don't include any of these in your tax return except the interest from the National Savings Bank or Trustee Savings Bank, which must be shown in full. Your taxable income includes gross earnings from your job and income (after tax) from such sources as building societies and dividends.

If self-employed, your taxable income is the income after tax from sources such as the profits of your accounting year which ended in the last tax year.

If, having been employed, you have lost your job so that you are no longer liable to pay income tax, and you have a mortgage, you should advise your building society immediately and call at the Social Security Office to obtain their help and advice.

843 Income tax (2)
When is the best date to marry, tax-wise? If the bride has an investment income of any size, the couple would probably be better off (moral issues aside) living together, unmarried, because — if they marry — her income will be added to that of her husband, which will increase his tax liability. Otherwise, the wedding date depends on the wife's earned income (assuming the husband earns a reasonable wage).

If she earns double the basic personal allowance (total income), the couple should marry as soon as she has earned her basic personal allowance within the tax year, regardless of whether or not she is going to continue to work after marriage.

If she earns over the basic allowance but less than twice as much, and she is going to carry on working, fix the date so that she can earn her basic allowance *after* marriage but before the end of the tax year. But if she is going to stop working, marry as soon as she has earned the basic allowance.

If she earns just the basic allowance or less, the couple should marry after 5th April and before 6th May.

844 Income tax — personal reliefs
When you calculate your taxable income, you deduct personal reliefs from your total income. Be sure not to miss any, because you won't get them if you don't claim. These allow you some tax-free income. For example, a personal relief of £100 saves you £35.

845   Income tax – personal relief : married man
If you are a married man living with your wife, or if you are wholly and voluntarily maintaining your separated wife (there must be no legally binding agreement or court order for the payments), you get tax relief.

846   Income tax – personal relief : wife's earned income
If your wife earns an income, you get tax relief up to the amount of her earned income, to a maximum of £675. Thus, a wife can earn up to £675 each year without paying tax. This relief cannot be set off against her investment income. Nor does it apply if the couple have elected for the wife to be assessed on her earnings separately.

847   Income tax – personal relief : single persons
If you are single (or if you are married but not entitled to married man's relief), you are entitled to a tax allowance.

848   Income tax – personal relief : child relief
If you have a child (it may be an adopted one) living at any time in the tax year – or if you have custody of a child whom you maintain at your own expense throughout the tax year – you will be given tax allowance. There are three age categories for children : under 11, 11–15 inclusive, and 16 and over. The older the child, the larger the allowance. Children over 16 must be undergoing full-time education at an 'educational establishment' or full-time training for a trade, profession or vocation for at least two years. The allowance is reduced if the child receives income. Don't forget that the tax people won't know about the arrival of a new baby unless you tell them.

849   Income tax – personal relief : working child
If your child has a paper-round or earns money from investments, make sure that he earns less than £115 per year or it will affect your income tax. (Income Tax Child Allowance is reduced by £1 for every £1 of child's income in excess of £115.)

850   Income tax – personal relief : extra to child relief
If you are already entitled to child allowance or adopted child allowance for a child living with you, you may qualify for a further allowance. This is designed to help *either* someone who is already entitled to the single person's allowance *or* a married man whose wife is totally incapacitated throughout the tax year. This allowance is

available only to households in which no-one else is receiving housekeeper allowance because of the resident child.

851 Income tax – personal relief: housekeeper relief
If you are a widow or widower who has a female resident housekeeper (but no children for whom you are entitled to child relief), you may claim tax relief for her. But if she is a relative of yours, no-one else must claim relief for her.

852 Income tax – personal relief: daughter's services
If you are forced by old age or infirmity to depend upon the services of a daughter resident with you and maintained by you, you can claim tax relief. But you may not be able to get this as well as housekeeper relief if the subject of the claims is one and the same person. (A married man is not entitled to this allowance unless his wife is old and infirm.)

853 Income tax – personal relief: dependent relative
If you maintain your (or your wife's) dependent relative(s) at your own expense, you are entitled to relief. The relative(s) must *either* be your divorced, separated or widowed mother/father (or mother-in-law/father-in-law) *or* be unable to maintain themselves through old age or infirmity. If you are a single or separated woman, you get a higher rate of relief. The relief is reduced, £ by £, by the income of the relative(s) in excess of the basic retirement pension. The relative(s) does/do not have to live with the taxpayer.

854 Income tax – personal relief: blind people
If you or your husband/wife is a registered blind person, you are entitled to tax relief. Relief is reduced, £ by £, by any tax-free disability payment.

855 Income tax – personal relief: age allowance
A person aged 65 or over gets a tax-free allowance. Married people get a higher allowance. If total income exceeds £3,000, this allowance is reduced by £2 for every £3 of the excess until it is the same as the married man's allowance or single person's allowance, which it replaces.

856 Legal advice
The Law Society, which is the governing body for solicitors in England and Wales, publishes a number of useful leaflets. Write to: *The Law Society, The Law Society Hall, Chancery Lane, London WC1.*

857   Legal fees

Write to the *Legal Action Group, 28a Highgate Road, London NW5 1NS*, if you wish to bypass the legal profession. They will advise you whether any of the many Neighbourhood Law Centres are in your area. Or visit your local Citizen's Advice Bureau.

858   Legal fees – claims from retailers and manufacturers

Many people are discouraged from trying to get back their money (perhaps plus damages) from shops which have sold them faulty goods because they believe that legal costs will be far too high. They feel that, for a claim of less than, say, £30 or £40, it would simply not be worth going to court. If they but knew about it (and so long as they live in England or Wales), there is an easy way around this problem – it is quite a simple and inexpensive matter to bring a case oneself in the county court *without the aid of a solicitor.* If you were making a simple claim against a local shop, the procedure would be as follows :

1. Find the name and address of the local county court from your local phone directory (under 'courts').

2. Write (or type) a simple statement of the facts of your claim, stating the amount. You need three copies. This statement is called your 'particulars of claim'.

3. Visit the county court, taking the particulars of claim and any other relevant papers with you. Ask to see the court clerk. He will advise you on which kind of summons you need. You then complete a 'request form', including your own name and address and also that of the shop against which you are bringing the case.

4. You pay a fee, called a 'plaint fee', for the issuing of the summons. The size of the plaint fee depends upon the size of your claim and could be less than £1.

5. The court now issues and serves the summons.

6. If the shop pays up immediately, they also pay your plaint fee. If the case goes to trial and you win, the defendant (the shop) has to pay all your expenses as well as the plaint fee. If you lose the trial, you also lose the plaint fee. Depending upon the amount of your claim, you may also have to pay something towards the defendant's costs, but this will be a minimal amount. For example, if the claim were for not more than £5, you pay nothing. If the claim were for not more than £75, you would be unlikely to be asked to pay more than £3.

859   Legal fees – criminal court

If you have to face criminal charges, you do not have to have professional legal aid, although in most cases it is clearly wiser to do so. If you do decide to defend yourself, you should read Self-Defence in Court and the McKenzie Advisor, a leaflet available free from the Neighbourhood Law Centre, School of Law, University of Warwick, Coventry. You should send a stamped addressed envelope plus 1p for each extra copy required.

860   Legal fees – housing (1)

Selling a registered house without the aid of a solicitor is by no means difficult. Buying is rather more tricky, but you can still economise on your legal fees by: (a) going to your local reference library and looking up the article on 'Conveyancing Fees' which appeared in the June, 1975, issue of Which? magazine; (b) sending to the Subscription Department of The Consumers' Association, Caxton Hill, Hertford, for a copy of The Legal Side of Buying a House (which applies to England and Wales only and costs £1.75 including postage); (c) employing the services of the House Owners' Co-operative Ltd, 19 Sheepcote Road, Harrow, Middlesex (01-427 6218). The last named organisation will reduce your legal fees – probably to well under half the usual.

861   Legal fees – housing (2)

Send 60p (plus 11p for postage and packing) to Shelter, 86 Strand, London WC2, for a copy of their Housing Rights Handbook which gives invaluable information on all aspects of housing law. If you want individual help with your housing problems and live in London, ring Shelter Housing Aid Centre on 373 7276. Besides the Shelter Centres, there are scores of Housing Aid Centres (25 in London alone) run by local authorities, as well as a number of Catholic Housing Aid Centres. Look in your local telephone directory.

862   Legal fees – making a will

Read Wills and Probate, obtainable from the Subscription Department of The Consumers' Association, Caxton Hill, Hertford, price £1.40 including postage.

863   Legal fees – Social Security claims

Anyone wanting information on their Social Security entitlement should write to the East London Claimants'

Union, Dame Colet House, Ben Johnson Road, London E1. Also, there is a helpful booklet, *National Welfare Benefits Handbook*, published by the *Child Poverty Action Group, 1 Macklin Street, London WC2*, costing 30p.

For allowances not connected with national insurance, read *The Penguin Guide to Supplementary Benefits*, compiled by Tony Lynes.

The Citizen's Rights Office, 1 Macklin Street, London WC2, will represent you at tribunals, free of charge, if they take up your case for you.

864   Legal fees – solicitor's
If you do use a solicitor, remember that most of his fees are controlled. If you think his bill is rather high, you can have it checked. If the fees under question relate to a court case, ask the court to check them. If the fees do not relate to a court case (conveyancing, probate, etc.) ask your solicitor to obtain a certificate from the Law Society verifying that they are correct.

865   Low-paid workers' benefits
There is a whole range of benefits for people on low income – free medical and dental prescriptions, free milk, free vitamins for expectant and nursing mothers, free school meals and help towards the cost of school uniforms, free travel to hospital for treatment and free legal aid. Some of these are also available for people on supplementary and other benefits. All of them are described in the *Family Income Supplement* leaflet. Information from Social Security Office.

866   Low-paid workers' family income supplement
A low-paid worker with a family can claim the following from Social Security: up to £7 per week for families with one child; up to £7.50 per week for families with two children; up to £8 per week for families with three children; rising by 50p for each additional child. It is believed that only about half of the families who are eligible for benefit have claimed for it. A single parent with a child may also claim if his or her earnings are not very high. Information from Social Security Office.

867   Milk – free
If you have two children under school age and are expecting a third, congratulations – you are entitled to a free pint of milk per day! Ask at Social Security Office.

868 Phone bills
Some local authorities will pay the telephone rental charges for housebound and disabled people.

869 Professional representation
If an authority is trying to purchase your house compulsorily – perhaps for a road-widening scheme – do not try to fight the case yourself or go to a legal aid solicitor. Instead you can make the authority pay the fees for a solicitor, estate agent or surveyor to represent you. (For details of further aspects, read the booklet *Public Inquiries into Road Proposals*, published by the Department of the Environment.)

870 Rates (1)
A rates rebate (depending on your earnings, the size of your family and the amount of your rates) is available to people who own their own houses, to tenants who also pay rates, and to tenants (including council tenants) who pay rates as a part of their rent. About one million people entitled to this relief have not asked for it. Information from Council Offices.

871 Rates (2)
Ask your council whether they give any discount for payment of rates a year in advance. Some allow 2%.

872 Rates (3)
Did you know that some councils give temporary rate reductions for temporary inconveniences, like major road works?

873 Rent – council tenants
Council tenants who cannot afford to pay the full rent because of family size or insufficient income may obtain a rent rebate. Information from Council Offices.

874 Rent – private tenants
Might you be paying too high a rent? Local authorities do not take into account the laws of supply and demand when assessing what is a fair rent. Therefore, if you are paying a high rent in a popular area, the local authority might rule that you are paying too much, in which case your landlord would be obliged to give a reduction.*

(*A private tenant and a housing association tenant would receive a rent allowance in cash. A council tenant would receive a rebate – i.e. a reduction in his rent.)

Also, your income, family size and amount of rent may qualify you for a rent rebate or allowance. Contact your local Council Offices.

875 Sickness

No apology is made for including 'sickness benefit' because so many people lose their allowance by not claiming or by claiming incorrectly. If you are employed (or self-employed) and paying full-rate National Insurance Contributions and you are prevented from working by illness, you are entitled to claim. Benefits are similar to those for the unemployed. If illness lasts more than 28 weeks, then 'invalidity benefit' is paid. But you *must* obtain a National Insurance medical certificate from your doctor and you *must* send it to the Social Security Office within six days of first being absent from work, or 21 days if it is the first time you have claimed. Supporting certificates must also be supplied for as long as the illness lasts. If you wait before doing this, you may well lose all or part of your benefit. Information from Social Security Office.

876 Widow's allowance

When a husband dies, his widow (providing she is under the age of 60) is entitled to a 'widow's allowance' for 26 weeks — but only if the husband made the required number of National Insurance payments. Information from Social Security Office.

877 Widow's pension

If a widow is over 50 years of age when her husband dies, or when her other allowances end, she is entitled to a pension (providing her husband's National Insurance payments were satisfactory). If she is between 40 and 50 when he dies or when her entitlement to 'widowed mother's allowance' (see no. 879) ceases, she receives an age-related widow's pension, which is at a lower rate. She must claim within three months of her husband's death. Information from Social Security Office.

878 Widow's supplementary allowance

A widow may be granted a supplementary allowance for up to 26 weeks based upon her husband's earnings during the tax year which ended before the first Monday of the year in which the claim is made. Information from Social Security Office.

879 Widow with children

A 'widowed mother's allowance' is available. Its size depends upon the number of children and it applies for as long as the children are receiving full-time education or apprenticeship training and are under 19 years of age. Information from Social Security Office.

How to save money on
Motoring

880 Accidents
If you are involved in an accident and are confident that you were in no way to blame, grab any independent witnesses before they disappear and take their names and addresses (and registration numbers, if in cars). One or two witnesses could be a big help to you. Be persistent in pressing your claim. Get a solicitor to write letters on your behalf.

881 Anti-freeze
Make your own by mixing glycerine and water. One part glycerine to 4 parts water will give you protection down to −5°C. By mixing 2 parts glycerine to 3 parts water, protection will be extended down to −15°C.

882 Buying a car (1)
If you are a driver who lives in the middle of a city and needs a car only occasionally, you do not need to own one. Remember, running a car today costs over £600 per annum. So hire – and save money!

883 Buying a car (2)
When buying a car from a dealer, do not sell him your old one if you can possibly sell it privately. A dealer has to re-sell your car, so his best offer will be about 20–25% below his resale price. You could probably get that additional 20–25% from a private buyer.

884 Buying a car (3)
It is wise to remember that a car depreciates most during its first two years of life. Therefore, from the point of view of economy, it is advisable to buy a car at least two years old. By choosing carefully, and by always looking after the car, it is possible even to re-sell at a profit.

885 Buying a new car (1)
Never pay cash for a straight-off-the-assembly-line new car without getting at least 10% off the dealer's purchase price.

886 Buying a new car (2)
Don't make the common mistake of buying a car which is larger than you need. All right, so you want to take the wife and children on their annual tour of Scotland! If you buy a much smaller car (which will be big enough for your motoring needs during the other 50 weeks of the year), you can hire a bigger car for the holidays – and still save yourself £200–£300 per annum.

887 Buying a used car (1)
In order not to buy a heap, you must either (a) buy from a reputable dealer who will give a guarantee, or (b) have the car checked mechanically – either by a friend with a sound knowledge of engines or by the AA or RAC (both of which make a charge of around £8 for a thorough – and very worthwhile – inspection).

888 Buying a used car (2)
Watch out for the big VAT fiddle! When you buy a used car (or any other second-hand goods) from a dealer, you should pay VAT *only on his profit margin*, not on the selling price. For example, if a new car costs £1,000, and VAT is 8%, the price you pay will be £1,080. But a second-hand car selling at £1,000 would have only £14.81 added on for VAT if the dealer paid £800 for it. Of course, if you buy privately, there is no VAT.

889 Buying a used car (3)
Remember that second-hand car 'bargains' – along with Santa Claus and fairies – do not exist. Everyone – dealers and private sellers alike – knows the normal going price for any car being sold. Therefore, if a vehicle is offered at a very cheap price, there is definitely something wrong with it.

890 Car maintenance (1)
As garage labour is now so expensive, you can save a lot of money by doing simple servicing jobs for yourself. The manual for your car should explain how to check the electrical equipment, clean or replace sparking plugs, change wiper blades or lamp bulbs, etc.

891 Car maintenance (2)
One of the biggest causes of depreciation of your car is corrosion. You can prevent it by washing your car thoroughly at least once a fortnight. Use a hose to clear

mud and grit from underneath. Do this regularly, especially in winter.

892 Chrome
Before going on a sea-side motoring holiday, don't forget to wipe over all the chrome with chrome cleaner – and leave it on. Repeat during the holiday, again leaving the chrome cleaner on. Sea air is much more corrosive than the kind you breathe at home. It can cause pounds' worth of damage in one or two weeks. Better to have your chrome temporarily dulled by dried-on chrome cleaner than peeled off by rust.

893 Garaging car at airport
If you are taking a plane flight and plan to garage your car at the airport, or at any of the garages near the airport – don't! The charges are ridiculous. If you can find a small bed-and-breakfast place near the airport, their parking charge will be far more realistic.

894 Insurance (1)
Is your car worth its insurance? There is no point in paying a comprehensive cover for an elderly heap. But you do need to be covered for third party claims, as well as having the basic cover required by law.

895 Insurance (2)
There are four ways in which you may cut the cost of a fully comprehensive policy: (a) By voluntarily bearing the first part (say, £25 or £50) of each and every claim resulting from accident repair costs. (This is well worth doing because, in any case, you would probably rather pay for small claims than lose your no-claim discount.) (b) By changing from comprehensive to third party, fire and theft (or even to third party only). (c) By restricting the policy to cover only one or two named people. (d) By changing your car for one with a lower insurance rating.

896 Insurance (3)
Special, cheaper policies providing restricted cover are available from some insurance companies. To qualify, you must: be over 25 (or 30), under 65 (or 70); have not claimed for three (or five) years; be in a low-risk job; have no convictions other than parking offences or one speeding offence over the previous five (or ten) years; not have a high-risk car; drive for pleasure/personal business only.

897   Insurance (4)

Some insurers – but not many – issue 'agreed value' policies. This means that they assess the value of your car at the beginning of each year of insurance. If your car is an accident 'write off', the agreed value is immediately paid.

898   Insurance (5)

Do not make the false economy of insuring with a cut-price company. Remember how many of these have collapsed in the past, leaving a mass of debts and thousands of unprotected policy holders. Write to one of the following for a list of their members within your area:

Association of Insurance Brokers, Craven House, 121 Kingsway, London WC2B 6PD.

The Corporation of Insurance Brokers, 15 St. Helen's Place, London EC3A 6D5.

Lloyds Insurance Brokers' Association, Lloyds Building, Line Street, London EC3M 7DQ.

899   Insurance (6)

Did you know that you can save 5–10% on the premiums of two or more cars by insuring them on the same policy? And that you may qualify for a combined discount of 20–25% if you also limit the number of drivers?

900   Motoring abroad – petrol and other concessions

If you are a member of the RAC or AA, and planning to take your car abroad, be sure to ask them what concessions are available to you. For example, if you are going to Italy you can obtain cut-price petrol coupons or a Museum Card which entitles you to up to a 50% reduction on the entry fees for museums and art galleries. If you are not an RAC or AA member, enquire at the National Tourist Offices, in London, of the countries you are visiting.

901   Oil

The only way to save money on engine oil is by buying it in bulk at discount prices. But the oil must be the one recommended for the car, must be new (not cleaned) and you must store it well to keep it clean. Inferior or dirty oil could cost you plenty in the long run.

902   Optional extras

If you are buying a *new* car, you pay about an extra 10% in VAT and car tax upon all the optional extras fitted before delivery. Therefore, you can save money by buying the car without the extras and fitting them yourself. Even if you pay a garage to fit them, you will make a slight saving.

903 Petrol (1)

If you are a little lazy and use the car for short journeys, it is worth bearing in mind that the initial starting of the car eats up the petrol more than anything else. A car which normally does a respectable 30 mpg may achieve less than 10 mpg over a run to the newsagent's.

904 Petrol (2)

Are you one of those drivers who starts his engine five minutes before needed to let it warm up in the belief that greater efficiency will result? If so, you are wasting fuel – and possibly damaging the engine. The thing to do is to get the car moving and go through the gears as soon as decently possible. This will get the engine functioning at peak temperature, which saves petrol.

905 Petrol (3)

A nippy start with high revving in the gears wastes petrol. Move away smoothly and steadily with normal usage of each gear.

906 Petrol (4)

When you drive with your choke out, you get only about seven miles to the gallon.

907 Petrol (5)

A very useful clue to wasteful driving is noise – noisy gear changing, noisy breaking and noisy acceleration. Quiet driving is economical driving.

908 Petrol (6)

When on a run avoid high speeds, excessive use of the choke, sudden acceleration, hills and bad traffic conditions, all of which increase petrol consumption, sometimes by 100%. When going off for your holiday, it makes sense to drive at night when traffic conditions are so much easier.

909 Petrol (7)

On hot days park in the shade to avoid petrol loss by evaporation.

910 Petrol (8)

Avoid all petrol stations offering gift stamps – they usually add a penny or two to the cost of each gallon.

911 Petrol (9)

Don't buy petrol with too low an octane rating – it could cause engine damage. But don't waste money by using petrol with too high a rating. Try the grade one star less than recommended by the manufacturers, who are often too pessimistic in these matters. Over half the cars in Britain would be perfectly happy with three star fuel. If you make the switch and find that the engine knocks or tends to continue running for a moment or so after switching off, you can still compromise by filling up half with the recommended grade and half with the lower one.

912 Petrol (10)

Keep sparking plugs clean or your petrol consumption will rise.

913 Petrol (11)

If your tyres are under-inflated, more petrol is needed by the engine to move the car along. But don't be greedy and over-inflate your tyres or you may have an accident.

914 Petrol (12)

Overloading the car or towing another vehicle both increase petrol consumption. Don't do either unnecessarily.

915 Petrol (13)

Petrol deteriorates and becomes less efficient if stored too long. So, if you like to keep a gallon of petrol handy in a can, make sure you pour it into the tank and replace with fresh juice at regular, short intervals.

916 Petrol (14)

Even an *empty* roof rack increases petrol consumption and a badly packed roof rack can do so by as much as 25%. You can minimise wind resistance by placing cases flat, never standing up, wrapping with tarpaulin or plastic (well tucked in), and tying with rope.

917 Petrol (15)

In very cold weather, blank off part of the radiator with aluminium foil. A hot engine is more efficient than a cool one.

918 Petrol (16)

When motoring along a hilly road – and road conditions, visibility and speed restrictions allow – speed downhill fast enough to 'freewheel' up the next hill. You need only half as much petrol to accelerate downhill as you do uphill.

919 Petrol (17)
To reach top engine temperature (and peak performance) more quickly, you could fit: a radiator blind; an electrical fan (thermostatically controlled); a variable pitch fan; or a block immersion heater. But do not forget that all savings made on petrol need to be offset against the initial cost of buying and installing the unit, so that it is very doubtful whether one would make an overall economy. A professional car mechanic gives the opinion that only the last device — the block immersion heater — would make any appreciable saving, and then only if the car were much used for short distance, stop-start motoring, like frequent shopping expeditions.

920 Petrol (18)
If you don't drive too close to the vehicle in front, you will be better able to maintain an even speed and you won't need to change gear or brake so often.

921 Petrol (19)
There is a much quoted myth that you can save petrol by using engine oil of a grade or two heavier than recommended, thus making your engine run more economically. Don't believe it! You should use only the grade of oil recommended. If your car is so old that it *needs* a very heavy oil, the chances are that it shouldn't be on the road at all.

922 Petrol (20)
Have your wheel alignments checked at least every six months and check your tyre pressure every two weeks. Also, make sure that your engine is tuned correctly.

923 Petrol (21)
At the end of the day, always *back* your car into the garage. This will ensure that the awkward manoeuvring is done with a warm engine, at night — not with a cold engine, in the morning.

924 Road fund licence
You can save yourself £3.95 per year by having the car taxed by the year (£40) instead of every four months (which totals £43.95).

925 Selling your car (1)

There are three ways you may do this – privately, to a dealer, and by auction. The private sale will bring you the best price, but the question is : how to advertise as cheaply as possible ? Advertising in large circulation newspapers can be expensive. It is normally much cheaper to invest about £3 or £4 in a local 'computer car club'. They will circulate buying and selling lists within 100 miles of your home. You will find a registration form in most of the motoring magazines.

926 Selling your car (2)

You will get a better price for your car if you sell it just before reaching one of the magic ten-thousand mile figures – e.g. when it has done just under 30,000 miles, not just over.

927 Selling your car (3)

Don't deceive yourself that people will recognise the quality of your car, even under a layer of dirt. People really do judge by appearances and you can sometimes add 10% to the value of a car by giving it a good wash and polish.

928 Servicing charges

Instead of paying your garage a heavy fee to check over the steering, brakes or suspension, you can save money by going to a specialist in, say, the braking system. Besides looking at your car with his own speciality in mind, he will probably give it a general inspection (on request) for no extra charge.

929 Spare parts

Enormous savings can be made on spare parts by purchasing them from breakers' yards. Such items as trim bits, door panels, suspension parts, prop-shafts, lamp units, wheels and brake drums may be bought very cheaply. But never get your tyres in this way – you could be buying trouble. Incidentally, it is wise to choose parts from a crashed car rather than from one that has died of rust and neglect.

930 Tyres (1)

If you do a low annual mileage, you may as well settle for cross-ply tyres, which are cheaper than radials. But if your year's mileage is high, radial-ply tyres, with their much longer life, will prove more economical.

931 Tyres (2)
Lengthen the life of your tyres by running them in. When motoring on new ones, do not exceed 50 mph for the first 100 miles.

How to save money on
Shopping & Buying Methods

932 Bulk buying (1)
Everyone knows the advantage of bulk buying from discount stores, super stores or hypermarkets. But these places are not conveniently situated for everyone, and there is no point in spending a lot on petrol to reach one. Many people do not realise, however, that many small grocers are perfectly willing to buy in bulk from the wholesalers so that you may bulk buy from them. First, get to know your grocer as a regular customer, and then, when on friendly terms with him, ask whether he will do this.

933 Bulk buying (2)
Can't afford the initial outlay? It may be worth talking to your bank manager. It is quite likely that he would be willing to help you for what is really a long-term investment.

934 Bulk buying from farms
Many farmers let people pick and pay at very cheap prices. Ask the nearest office of the National Farmers Union for a list of local farms which do this.

935 Bulk buying of meat
The cheapest way of buying a whole slaughtered animal is to buy direct from the abattoir. If you are to avoid waste in the cutting up, expert cutting of the carcase is needed — and this is a skilled job. If anyone wishes to attempt it without the aid of a craftsman butcher, he should get leaflets on the cutting and preparation of different types of meat from: *The Meat & Livestock Commission, P.O. Box 44, Queensway House, Milton Keynes, Bucks.*

936 Bulk buying of vegetables
This may be done by the crate or sack from the large wholesale markets like Covent Garden. Of course, if you

live in the country, there may be a local market garden or orchard.

937 Buying meat, fish, poultry
When comparing costs in the shops, always think of the various foods in terms of so many *servings* per pound in weight. For example:

Lean meat, fish and poultry (without bones) give three–four servings per lb.

Chops, steaks of fish (with bone) and chicken portions give two–three.

Bony or fatty meats (chicken wings, spare ribs) give one–two.

By dividing the cost per lb by the number of servings per lb you can very easily estimate the cost per serving. Thus, if cod costs 60p per lb (three–four servings) and spare ribs cost 48p per lb (one–two servings), an average serving of cod costs $17\frac{1}{2}$p and an average serving of spare ribs 36p. So – surprisingly, cod is less than half the price (per serving) of spare ribs, although it costs more per lb.

938 Cash & carry
Consult your telephone directory's Yellow Pages to find the local cash & carry and discount stores and shop at them as much as possible. They can easily reduce your grocery bills by 15%. (If no bulk buying centres nearby, see no. 932.)

The Food Manufacturers' Federation Inc. investigates complaints about food if appeals to the retailer and manufacturers have failed to produce satisfaction. Write to: *The Food Manufacturers' Federation Inc., 1/2 Castle Lane, Buckingham Gate, London SW1E 6DN.*

939 Complaints against shopkeepers
Most problems can be sorted out by your local Consumer Advice Centre (see Yellow Pages). However, if your complaint is one covered by the Trade Descriptions Act – i.e. if it concerns short weight or measure in the supply of goods, incorrect description of goods, false claims, false trade descriptions, false promises regarding services or facilities, prices misquoted and false publicity – it should be dealt with by the local Trading Standards Office (or Consumer Protection Department as it is known in some areas). If you can't find the address in the tele-

phone directory, get it from your local government authority.

940 Consumer groups

If there is one in your area, join it! You will save the annual subscription many times over by shopping more efficiently and by knowing your rights when returning faulty goods to retailers. The address of your nearest local group is available from *The National Federation of Consumer Groups, 6 Valentine Road, Birmingham B14 7AJ.* (Enclose a stamped addressed envelope.)

941 Discount clubs

You will save many pounds per annum if you join a discount club. It costs a few pounds to join – about £3–£5 – but, with generous discounts on almost everything (up to 20% on some items), it does not take long to get back your subscription in terms of savings made. Some of these clubs issue 500-page catalogues listing just about everything that one needs to buy for house and garden, and including services like insurance or accountancy, all at greatly reduced prices.

942 Door-to-door salesmen

Always ask to see his credentials. If he doesn't have a card or letter of introduction, politely but firmly close the door. If he does, look in the telephone book to see if you can find the name of his firm. Bring the directory to the front door so that he can see what you are doing while he waits on the step. This will convince him that you're no cabbage. If the address is not a local one, find out whether the firm belongs to *Direct Sales and Service Association, 47 Windsor Road, Slough, Bucks* (Tel: 0753 31020). The Association lays down a code of conduct for its members, and usually knows what is going on and who is about. Be on your guard if a salesman tells you he is working for a research organisation or doing a survey, is from the education department or a student working for a scholarship or holiday. In nearly all cases such assertions amount to misrepresentation designed to get your confidence or sympathy. Do not ask the representative in. Tell him that you really don't have much time to spare, so could he please say what he has to say in about ten seconds. If whatever he is selling sounds: (a) just what you want; (b) is reasonably priced; and (c) is well guaranteed, tell him that you *might* be interested and ask him to call back when you will have a second opinion available. Do not sign anything.

Before the next meeting, check with your neighbours to see what they think. Have any of them bought the product? Check prices of competitive products in the shops, also their deferred payment charges.

When the salesman returns, get him to demonstrate the product fully. Also, ask him to explain price, guarantee and payment terms in full. Ask to see a copy of the agreement. Do not hesitate to say, 'Sorry, I can get better terms elsewhere', if that is the case. If you are still interested, thank the representative for giving you all the information and tell him that you now wish to talk it over with your husband/wife/budgerigar; would he please phone or call for your final decision at a specific time on the following evening? Then decide.

Never, never feel sorry for a door-to-door salesman — he may well earn more in one day than you and your family do in a week. And if you do buy something costing more than £30, by credit sale or on hire purchase, only to change your mind later, you have a legal 'cooling off period' of 72 hours during which you may opt out of the agreement, provided you did not sign it in a shop, showroom or office of a finance company.

Watch out for loan agreements. Until changes are brought about by the Consumer Credit Act*, such transactions are *not* subject to cancellation, and you will have to continue to pay even if the goods prove defective. Watch out, too, for rental or hire (not hire purchase) contracts where the goods never become your personal property.

943 Free goodies

It pays to complain! If you buy a dud film, write to the public relations officer of the film manufacturer — you will probably get two or three packets of film with a very courteous apology. If one of the raisins in your bar of chocolate turns out to be something sinister — and dead — take up your pen once more and you may well receive a few pounds of chocolate, by return. If products are not right, moan like mad!

(*The Consumer Credit Act, 1974, will be coming into force gradually over 1976/7.)

944 Fruit and vegetables

Make a fruit and vegetable calendar which will tell you which part of the year to expect each f and v to be at its cheapest. It is a good idea to enter, in red, on the same calendar the time of year when each is at its dearest (and most unbuyable!). This guide will be of especial value to you if you have a freezer or if you bottle items or make jam.

Here are the cheapest months, for a start:

FRUIT – cheapest months		FRUIT – cheapest months	
Apples		Limes	July–Feb
(cooking)	Aug–Dec	Lychees	Dec–Feb
Apples		Loganberries	July–Aug
(dessert)	Sept–Jan	Mandarins	Dec–Mar
Apricots	May–Aug	Mangoes	Jan–July
Avocado		Medlars	Nov–Dec
pears	Little change through year	Melons	June–Nov
Bananas	Little change through year	Oranges (except Sevilles)	Little change through year
Bilberries	July–Aug		
Blackberries	Sept–Oct	Passion fruit	Jan–Mar
Blackcurrants	July–Aug	Peaches	June–Sept
Cherries	June–Aug	Pears	Aug–Nov
Chinese		Plums	June–Oct
gooseberries	Sept–Dec	Pomegranates	Sept–Nov
Cranberries	Dec–Feb	Raspberries	June–Sept
Damsons	Aug–Oct	Redcurrants	June–Aug
Dates (fresh)	Oct–Mar	Rhubarb	April
Figs	Sept–Dec	Satsumas	Oct–Jan
Gooseberries	May–June	Seville	
Grapes	July–Nov	oranges	Dec–Mar
Greengages	July–Aug	Strawberries	June–Aug
Lemons	Nov–Feb	Tomatoes	June–Aug

VEG – cheapest months		VEG – cheapest months	
Artichokes		Kohl rabi . .	July–Oct
(globe) . .	July–Sept	Leeks	Nov–Mar
Artichokes		Lettuce . .	June–Aug
(Jerusalem) .	Jan–Apr	Mange-tout	
Asparagus . .	Jan–Mar	peas . .	June–Aug
Aubergines .	July–Oct	Marrows . .	Sept–Nov
Beetroot . .	Little change	Mushrooms	
	through year	(cultivated) .	Little change
Broad beans .	June–Aug		through year
Broccoli . .	Sept–May	Mushrooms	
Brussels		(field) . . .	Aug–Oct
sprouts . .	Nov–Feb	Onions . .	Sept–Dec
Cabbage . .	Little change	Parsley . .	Little change
	through year		through year
Capsicums .	July–Sept	Parsnips . . .	Oct–Mar
Carrots . . .	Jan–Aug	Peas	May–Aug
Cauliflower .	Sept–Nov	Potatoes	
Celeriac . .	Sept–Mar	(new) .	June–July
Celery	Dec–Apr	Pumpkin . .	Sept–Oct
Chicory . . .	Nov–Jan	Radish . . .	May–Aug
Chillis . . .	June–Aug	Runner	
Corn-on-the-		beans . .	July–Sept
cob . . .	Aug–Oct	Seakale . . .	Jan–Mar
Courgettes .	June–Aug	Spinach . .	Apr–July
Cucumber . .	July–Aug	Spring	
Endive . .	May–Aug	greens . .	Apr–July
Fennel . .	June–Oct	Swedes . . .	Dec–Mar
French		Turnips . . .	Dec–Mar
beans . .	June–Sept	Watercress . .	Jan–Feb
Garlic . . .	Little change		
	though year		

945 Furniture (1)

The cost of furniture can be depressing, particularly if you're setting up a home from scratch. Many people make the mistake of buying smart but inferior new furniture which looks quite good for a month or two but begins to disintegrate after a year or so. A more sensible procedure is to start by buying only one really good quality piece (perhaps a sofa) and to provide extra seating with elegant, but cheap, garden chairs. Matching armchairs can then be bought as funds allow, and the garden chairs can be transferred – to the garden.

946 Furniture (2)

One way that newly-marrieds can buy good quality **furniture** without **resorting** to **hire** purchase or bank robbery is to attend auctions at their local salesrooms. Here you can pick up nearly new furniture and carpets for only a few pounds. You should have a good nose around the auction room beforehand, noting the lots in which you are interested, and deciding upon the top limit you are prepared to pay — and having decided upon it, keep to it. It is wise to make this top limit an odd number just above an even one — £11, not £10 — as many people stop on the round figure.

947 Hire purchase/credit sale

When thinking of buying something on hp or credit sale, one point which you must check is whether you are to pay interest on the *entire* sum of money owing until the debt is repaid, or only on the *reducing balance* of the debt. The first method could cost you £20 more than the second on an item valued at £120. Argue about it, and you may get a change in the terms. If not, look elsewhere.

948 Home-making priorities

Setting up a home is a more formidable task than ever. Very few of us are lucky enough to be able to afford both a house *and* all the furniture. Which means that we have to decide on our priorities. When starting from scratch, the whole business can seem utterly confusing. The following priorities are suggested as guidelines with economy very much in mind.

First priority : get a place of your own if you possibly can. Living with in-laws or other relatives, no matter how well-meaning they are, puts a strain on any relationship.

Second : a good heating system of one sort or another.

Third : floor coverings and insulation in order to economise as much as possible upon Priority Two (see nos. 570–580).

Fourth : kitchen needs — sink unit, cooker, fridge, etc.

Fifth : a bed (which, to start with, could be a large slab of foam rubber).

Sixth : A TV set to keep you in touch with the outside world (you can buy old black and white ones for about £5).

949 House-buying

When viewing, it is wise to note the condition of the estate agent's 'For Sale' sign outside the house. Is it badly weathered? Has it been there a long time? If so, it is likely that the house owner is getting rather discouraged and might be ready to drop his price substantially. Haggle! And don't forget to look into the reason *why* the house has not sold – who knows, it might be falling apart!

950   Mail order catalogues (1)
In these inflationary days, it makes sense to buy expensive items on credit, provided (a) you do not take on more than you can afford, and (b) you are not charged for the credit. Thus, to pay over a number of months is to your advantage, because by the time the full debt has been paid the money will not be worth as much as it is today. In the meantime you could put the money to better use – by investments, for example.

951   Mail order catalogues (2)
There are many well advertised mail order catalogues which include some bargains, although many of their goods are far from cheap. One sure way of profiting from a mail order catalogue is to become a mail order agent, which means that by obtaining orders from your friends for goods in the catalogue you become entitled to 10% cash commission or the equivalent of $12\frac{1}{2}$% in the form of goods which you order for yourself. The time expended in running the agency is more than rewarded by the savings you make on the goods of your choice, and the convenience of being able to pay for the goods over several months.

952   Meat
You can lose money by insisting that your joint is lean. Fat is needed in the cooking to make the meat juicy and tender. Therefore, if there is no fat on your meat, you have to add some – at cost. And remember that the best meat does not have the fat wrapped around the outside like an overcoat; it has a speckled or 'marbled' effect, caused by thousands of tiny strands of fat showing through the lean. This meat should cook beautifully.

953   Potatoes
For a large family, it is economical to buy potatoes by the sack or half sack. They store well, especially in the dark – but do not leave them where frost can attack them. How far is the nearest farm?

954 Prices

Write to *The Consumers' Association, 14 Buckingham Street, London WC2N 6DS*, for the address of your nearest Consumers' Association Centre. From there you can obtain advice about complaints as well as information on local food prices.

955 Removals

If you need to sell your house and buy another in a different district, it may be worth placing a small ad. in the local newspaper of the town to which you are moving. By doing so, you might find someone wishing to move to your present home area who would be prepared to swop houses, enabling both parties to make several economies : you would avoid agent's fees, either completely or in part ; you would avoid stamp duty, which can amount to several hundred pounds ; and solicitor's costs would be much lower. Besides advertising, you could also use an estate agent and insist that he includes in his advertisements the words 'Owner moving to Town X. Would be interested in exchange'.

956 Removal costs (1)

If you live in Town A and want to move house to Town B, don't make the mistake of getting your quotations for removal costs from firms in Town A. If you do, they will be expensive because you will be expected to pay for the driver's wages and the petrol for the return journey. Instead, go to the Post Office and find a telephone directory for Town B. List the removal firms, and their telephone numbers. Ring them, asking whether they make deliveries from B to A. If so, they will be very happy to fit in your removal on the return journey – and the cost should be very reasonable.

957 Removal costs (2)

Another way of cutting removal costs is by finding a firm which can fit in your items, along with another removal, as a 'part load'.

958 Residents' associations

Members of a local residents' association usually get discounts from some local shops.

959 Sales

Most stores which have sales have a pre-sales viewing

day. It is advisable to attend this and to make a note of where any item is that you particularly want. Be there early on the opening day (are you game enough to camp on the pavement overnight?) and make straight for it.

960 Sandwich and vol-au-vent fillers
Supermarkets do their slicing of cold meats first thing in the morning. Inevitably, this produces many tiny scraps of meat which are too small to be included in the sliced meat packets – bits of ham, tongue, silverside, chicken and turkey – so they are mixed together and are sold off as cold meat pieces, sometimes at about 25% of the normal price. The most likely time to pick up one of these bargains is after the shop has been open for about one hour. Chopped up small, the pieces make tasty fillers for sandwiches or vol-au-vents.

961 Shopping
It is a fact proven by research that people in a cheerful frame of mind buy less than people who are feeling miserable. So cheer up! Try not to go shopping when you're feeling depressed because the danger is that you'll buy things to compensate for your misery. If you *must* go shopping when dejected, ask yourself when considering buying any item not on your shopping list whether you are doing so merely to give yourself a lift. If you are, be firm – resist the temptation and save the money.

962 Shopping at discount stores (1)
You can get genuine bargains at discount stores if you buy only the well-known branded goods. But ignore 'own label' or unknown brands – often these are specially manufactured for the discount store and are not worth even 1p more than the price asked. This applies especially to furniture and bedding.

963 Shopping at discount stores (2)
When you are considering buying a well-known branded product from a discount store, ignore the store's claim to be selling at so much below the manufacturer's recommended price. No doubt his claim is true, but possibly every other retailer in the town is also selling that product at below the recommended price. The only way to be sure is to shop around. Get a free, up-to-date catalogue from your discount store, note the things in which you are interested – and check the prices.

964   Shopping at self-service stores and markets

Shop as late as possible on a Saturday afternoon when buying perishables from a self-service store or a market. Prices often come tumbling down at this time because the market would rather sell it than store it. Similarly, you can find bargain priced perishables in supermarkets early on Monday mornings. There's nothing wrong with them – they have spent the weekend in the fridge – but they can no longer be sold as 'fresh'.

In the area in which the author lives, Thursday is the best day for meat and poultry. It may well be different in your part of the country, of course. The point is that different types of bargain occur on different days of the week. Therefore, if you switch your shopping days around, you should find new bargains on each day.

965   Shopping critically

If you can find fault with any article in a shop – a book with a torn page, a garment with a tiny flaw – you can probably haggle successfully for a good price reduction. It pays to be critical.

966   Shopping – discount for cash

Buying for hire purchase or credit sale is now so common that many ordinary (as distinct from 'discount') shops are perfectly happy to give a 'discount for cash payment' on more expensive items. If you start by negotiating for 10% off, you can usually get 5%. The author knows of one man who, by always buying in this way and never by hp, has saved several hundred pounds on normal selling prices over the years. Worthwhile discounts are available on electrical equipment, cameras, TV sets, watches, etc. For example, it is quite normal to get from 30% to 40% discount on record players. The places where you may get a discount off the list price are: ordinary shops in the High Street, departmental stores, electrical shops and electricity board showrooms; discount warehouses; discount mail order clubs (which you have to join, usually for a fee); mail order agencies. These all vary from area to area and it is impossible to say that any one of them gives a better deal than the others. The best procedure is: decide what product you wish to buy. Ignore the list price. Inspect local shops and stores and compare prices. Check the price at your local discount warehouse and also write to the discount mail order firms.

967 Shopping economically (1)
This one is only for the truly dedicated (and slightly masochistic) saver. Before going on a shopping expedition, estimate how much it should cost – and then take less with you!

968 Shopping economically (2)
Modern mass advertising and pre-packaging of goods make supermarkets and superstores possible. Because shoppers already know the products (from advertising) and because they are able to serve themselves (as the products are pre-wrapped), supermarkets are able to sell large quantities of goods while employing very few sales staff. This enables them to be generally cheaper than small self-service and ordinary counter service shops.

969 Shopping economically (3)
Although supermarket prices tend to be very reasonable over-all, it is worth keeping your eye on local greengrocers' prices which, unlike the supermarket, vary from day to day.

970 Shopping economically (4)
American research shows that hungry housewives buy more than housewives who have just eaten. If you have not eaten within two hours before shopping, you are much more likely to be attracted by the packages of food, so make sure you shop not too long after a meal!

971 Shopping economically (5)
It is a tested fact that the less frequently you shop, the less you will buy. Infrequent shopping means fewer opportunities for expensive impulse buying or fill-in buying. Once-a-week shopping should be the maximum. The main 'basic shopping' should be done in large quantities once per month.

972 Shopping economically (6)
Research indicates that a housewife shopping with her husband or child tends to buy more. So shop alone, if possible.

973 Shopping economically (7)
Try not to touch any item unless you intend to buy it. Research reveals that, once you have handled a product, there is a 50–50 chance that you will buy it, whether you need it or not. That is why some supermarkets stick the

little price label on the 'awkward' side of the pack – where you can't see it without picking up the box.

974 Shopping economically (8)
Be sure to look at the lower shelves – that's where the bargains are! Because retailers know that there is a natural tendency to buy the products at eye level, they position their high-profit items there.

975 Shopping economically (9)
Never take savings for granted. Some convenience foods are cheaper as well as easier. Always check. For example, you would expect sliced beetroot, bottled in vinegar, to be more expensive than unprepared whole beets, but this is not always the case. The economies made by mass growing, mass processing, mass bottling, mass distributing and mass selling bottled beetroot mean that they can be sold at a lower cost per pound of vegetable than the whole beet. Which also means that you are saved the cost of vinegar and bottling time. Another example: 1 lb of frozen peas costs less to buy than the 3 lb of peas in the pod that are necessary to produce that 1 lb.

976 Shopping economically (10)
Beware of products that come to you in 'sets' or 'handypacks'. Take breakfast cereals as an example. It is true, of course, that the special pack offers convenience and/or variety. But you are paying for that convenience – dearly! You may be getting less than 40% of the cereal which you would obtain by spending the same amount of money on a large carton of just one type of cereal.

977 Shopping for bananas
If you wish to buy your bananas cheaply (maybe at less than half price), ask your greengrocer whether he has a 'loose banana box'. For some inexplicable reason, most people will buy bananas only if attached to other bananas. Which means that the shopkeeper would be left with a number of unwanted, solitary bananas if he were not prepared to sell them off cheaply.

978 Shopping for dates
Large, well-shaped dates are displayed attractively in boxes and sold as 'dessert dates'. Smaller, less handsome dates are pressed together into blocks and sold as 'cooking dates' – at half the price and tasting just the same.

979 Shopping for fish
Certain fish are at their best and their cheapest at certain seasons. Mackerel (April to early July) is a very nourishing, tasty fish. Herrings are at their juiciest and cheapest during May and June. The best time for sprats is from October to March.

980 Shopping for grapes
Did you know that grapes, like bananas (see no. 977), may be bought loose at a much reduced price? Who's going to know the difference once they've been popped into a fruit salad or a grape jelly?

981 Shopping for lemons
When the price of lemons becomes ridiculous — as it does each year — it is cheaper to buy bottled lemon juice.

982 Shopping for lettuce
Never buy a lettuce that has had its outer leaves removed — it probably isn't very fresh. Also, those outside leaves (which many people throw away) are excellent for soups.

983 Shopping for food (1)
You can get maximum value for money by taking along a simple, handy cookbook when you go to the supermarket or grocer's. There is not much point in finding some type of food at a bargain price if you don't snap it up because you can't think of what you can do with it. A quick dip into your cookbook could remind you of a suitable dish.

984 Shopping for food (2)
If you have plenty of storage space, it makes good sense to buy food in bulk — and more cheaply — so long as it is non-perishable and provided that you do not fall into the trap of increasing your usage because 'there is plenty more in the store'. Most tinned foods may be bought by the crate at considerable savings. Watch your local newspaper for offers. If you cannot afford the initial outlay, why not group together with nearby friends?

985 Shopping for food (3)
It pays to shop around, if you have the time and energy. If you compare prices in stores and markets for a few weeks, you will soon learn which places to avoid for certain lines and where to expect genuine bargains. But don't expect to find one shop which is cheaper for

everything. You cannot shop with real economy unless you select different items from two or three shops.

986   Shopping for mushrooms
Mushroom stalks, which cost less than half the price of mushrooms, are just as delicious, just as nutritious.

987   Shopping for food (4)
Choosing the supermarkets' 'own brands' in preference to the well known ones usually makes a saving of over 5% without any loss in quality. This is because 'own brands' carry very low distribution costs.

988   Shopping for food (5)
When shopping in supermarkets, it is not enough to compare the cost prices of articles without also considering the net weight. However, very often – as in the case of biscuits – there are hardly two brands selling the same weight, which makes a comparison of quantities-for-money difficult. The best way to check is by dividing the price by the number of ounces (or grams or millilitres). Thus, if product A weighs 40 grams and is priced at 21p, it is costing you .52p per gram (21p÷40). If brand B costs 30p for 60 grams, it is fractionally cheaper (30p÷60=.5p per gram).

A pocket electronic calculator is a wonderful help when shopping in this way and also enables you to keep a running total and, finally, to check the addition of your bill (see nos. 998 & 999). Although they cost anything from £5 upwards, one would eventually pay for itself by helping you always to obtain full value for money, and to avoid errors.

989   Shopping for grapefruit
You can often get a bargain in grapefruit by going for the ones with ugly, discoloured skins, sometimes with brown blobs. These tend to be cheaper because of their off-putting appearance. Be guided by the firmness of feel of the fruit in the hand.

990   Shopping for oranges, lemons or grapefruit (1)
When buying an orange, a lemon or a grapefruit, choose for weight, not size. A small fruit may have thick skin – and therefore less flesh than it would appear to have.

991   Shopping for oranges, lemons and grapefruit (2)
Oranges, lemons and grapefruit vary considerably in price

through the year. Yet not many people think of freezing them when they are cheap.

992 Shopping for soft fruit
If you live in the country, save money by shopping late in the day for soft fruits, either at the fruiterer's or at the roadside stall, where home-grown produce is for sale.

993 Shopping for tomatoes
When cooking tomatoes are at their most expensive, it's cheaper to buy tinned ones. Also, very small salad tomatoes are cheaper than normal size ones, besides having more flavour.

994 Shopping for vitamin C drinks
Never buy a bottle of orange juice or any other 'vitamin C' drink which has been standing in the sunlight. Sunshine kills the vitamin C quicker than anything and a bottle of orange squash which has been exposed to sunshine for several hours is not much better than a bottle of sweet water.

995 Shopping – getting your money back
Ignore notices in shops which say 'No money back' or 'No goods exchanged' ; if you are sold a defective product, you are legally entitled to have your money returned. The shopkeeper may try to persuade you to accept a credit note. If you do so, you give up your right to have your money back and cannot change your mind later. Of course, if you know that the original purchase was a mistake of yours, it is only fair to accept a credit note.

996 Shopping in the West End
During the October–January period of the past few years, British Rail have provided a shopping scheme for people living in the South East. They have sold special cheap rate train tickets (linked to the Awayday Scheme – see no. 1027) which come with a free book of shopping vouchers entitling the purchaser to discounts of up to 10% in over 40 West End stores, shops and restaurants. These tickets were available at most stations in London and the South East. If you live in this seemingly privileged part of the country and would like to take advantage of such a useful money-saver, enquire at your local railway station (or direct to British Rail) to see if the same scheme will be in operation next October–January – there's every chance it will be.

997 Shopping list

When you have written out your shopping list, read through it again, this time jotting an N against each of the needs and a W against each of the wants. Then cross out all the items marked W.

998 Shopping – mistakes (1)

A recent survey carried out by *Which?* magazine indicated that about half the bills rung up by supermarkets were wrong, sometimes favouring themselves and sometimes the customer. There are two practical ways of combating this: If you have an electronic calculator, you can 'ring up' the prices on it as you put each item into your wire basket. Alternatively, you can check every price when you get home and tell the store immediately if they have made a mistake.

999 Shopping – mistakes (2)

An alarming number of mistakes are caused by the checkout girls being unaware of price reductions. So, if you buy a product that is reduced, make sure it is rung up correctly.

1000 Shopping – special offers

Never buy an item marked 'special offer' or '4p off' unless you have checked its cost per ounce against the costs per ounce of its competitors. If the retailer knocks 4p off the price of an expensive product, it may still be dearer than a cheaper, but equally good, product at its full price.

1001 *Which?* magazine

Before purchasing any expensive item it is wise to see what The Consumers' Association's *Which?* magazine has had to say about it. Ask at your local library to see the *Which?* index so that you can track down the issue which deals with the item in which you are interested.

How to save money on
Travel
& Holidays

1002   Air travel (1)
Anyone booking a flight to the USA, Canada or the Caribbean can do so at considerably reduced fare as an 'Advanced Booking Charter Flight'. To qualify, they must book at least 60 days in advance and stay abroad for a minimum of a fortnight (or ten days if you leave after 31st October and return before 1st April). Cheaper fares are available for other destinations as 'affinity charters' by belonging to a chartering club for at least six months before flying. (A useful leaflet is available from the *Civil Aviation Authority, Room 356, Aviation House, 129 Kingsway, London WC2B 6NN.*)

1003   Air travel (2)
Air Purchase Excursions (APEX) fly the Atlantic route using scheduled aircraft, not chartered, so there are more places available. However, their charges are higher than ABC's (see no. 1002) and their conditions include staying abroad for at least 22 days.

1004   Air travel (3)
Excursion flights are cheaper than full price, but not so cheap as APEX (see no. 1003). There are 14–21 day and 22–45 day excursions.

1005   Air travel (4)
Youth and student fares have ended, but parties of ten or more may negotiate cheaper rates through International Air Transport Association agents. You might get as much as 25% off.

1006   Air travel (5)
You can get cheap rates from travel agents. Some charter part, or all, of an aircraft, taking the risk of non-sale of

tickets themselves, and sell the tickets at cheap rates. Others buy block bookings at economic rates and sell off the tickets separately. The advantage of booking with a travel agent is that you can get a cheap ticket without booking a long time in advance.

1007 Air travel (6)
It's financially safer to buy your air tickets from an agent with an Air Travel Organisers' Licence (ATOL) number, issued by the Civil Aviation Authority. He has bonded a percentage of his turnover to ensure that his travellers abroad can be flown home if there is any trouble.

1008 Air travel (7)
Before borrowing money to take a holiday or to travel by air, remember that the cheapest way is by bank loan.

1009 Bus travel (1)
Have you checked the fare stages? You might save 3p by walking on one stop – and feel fitter.

1010 Bus travel (2)
If you spend 20p per day on bus travel (10p each way), five days per week, you are spending about £50 per year in this way. So, you could buy a bicycle for £30 and save £20 in the first year and £50 (or more, as fares rise) in each following year.

1011 Children's travel
Some holiday tour companies offer special cheap rates for children travelling with one parent at certain times of the year.

1012 French food (1)
When on a touring holiday in France it is possible to spend a fortune upon meals, for French food is very expensive by British standards. One way to avoid this, of course, would be to take plenty of tinned food with you. But this is far from satisfactory, partly because of the inconvenience of transporting all those tins, partly because of the nuisance of having to prepare all your own meals – but most of all because of the sheer frustration of touring what is probably the best fed country in the world on a monotonous diet of prefabricated soup and baked beans. Therefore, the following compromise is suggested. Take some rations with you, yes, but only for the mid-day snack (following a light, Continental breakfast). This will mean that, by the

evening, you will probably be nicely ravenous and ready to enjoy the wonderful French food. You may do so relatively inexpensively by avoiding all hotels and restaurants and, instead, eating at a place which you would probably avoid in Britain – the lorry drivers' pull-up. These are scattered all over France and are distinguished by a circular sign, half red and half either blue or green, with the words 'Les Routiers' across the middle, usually in yellow. The thing to remember is that, while no-one eats badly in France, some eat less expensively than others. In Les Routiers, you will find beautifully prepared food in clean, simple surroundings at very reasonable prices. They also provide cheap accommodation in the same style.

1013 French food (2)

If you do decide to 'splash out' on the occasional meal in a conventional French restaurant, choose your days carefully, remembering that most French restaurants put up their fixed price menus by about 5F (55p) on Saturdays and Sundays.

1014 Holiday – cheap (1)

The cheapest holiday is a camping holiday, but not if you *buy* all the gear – new frame-tent, beds, sleeping bags, etc. Anyway, it is wiser to *try* camping first, to make sure you take to the outdoor life. One solution is to borrow a friend's camping equipment. Don't be shy – many campers start by doing this and most experienced campers would rather have their equipment in use than piled up in the loft. Alternatively, you can hire camping equipment at very reasonable rates from most camping shops. Or you could buy a very good second-hand frame-tent from one of the firms who hire them out. Usually, they hire out tents for only one season and then sell them off before replacing with next year's model.

If you are touring on the Continent by car, remember that many of the car ferry firms (e.g. Sealink, Townsend, Thorensen and Normandy) hire out camping equipment at cut-price rates.

1015 Holiday – cheap (2)

The second cheapest 'normal' holiday is the self-catering flat, caravan or cottage, preferably out of season. Cottages usually sleep about six people, so, if you have friends whom you could bear to be with right through your holidays (and there is no tougher test of friendship), why not join forces and save money?

1016   Holiday – cheap (3)
You can economise on holidays by going away for one week less than usual and spending the other week being entertained (inexpensively) in your home town. This is especially feasible if you have children. Check with the local town hall. You'll be surprised how many things to do there are costing little or nothing.

1017   Holiday – cheap (4)
If you are fortunate enough to have flexible holiday dates – and if you are not too rigid about where you wish to holiday – you can snap up a cheap bargain by waiting for the special offers, usually bookable one month before departure. These are package holidays which the tour operators have failed to sell at the full price, sometimes of normal duration and sometimes quite short, like five days. Watch the travel pages of the national newspapers for announcements.

1018   Holiday exchange
If you can bring yourself to take the risk (and if you live in a resort), you can have a very cheap holiday by swopping houses for two or three weeks with a family living in a different resort. Your family and theirs should be comparable in as many ways as possible; for example, they should have the same number of children and, ideally, similarly rated houses. Most people who make this arrangement are so anxious to be fair to the other family that they go to extreme lengths to leave their host's house spick and span. But there is always the danger of being unlucky, so, if you are a natural worrier, forget this one. If you *are* interested, however, the cheapest way of making contact with somebody is by putting a small ad. in the weekly newspaper of the chosen resort. You could find the paper's name and address by reference to the telephone directory at your Post Office. It is advisable to advertise well in advance – say, in the January prior to the summer. If you prefer to have the whole thing arranged for you, write to: *Home Interchange, 19 Bolton Street, Piccadilly, London W1*. Of course, this will cost more than if you make the arrangements yourself.

1019   Holiday food
Have you noticed how much more expensive food is at holiday resort shops ? If you are going to such a place on a camping or self-catering holiday, the message is clear – take as much food as possible with you ! Even though you will use a little more petrol (because of the extra weight), you should still make an over-all saving.

1020   Holidays
Avoid holidays during the high season of July and August, if you possibly can – it's more expensive. If you *must* go at that time, try to avoid the overcrowded, over-priced holiday resorts.

1021   Holidays – winter
Cut-price, out-of-season holidays are available from hotels who would rather make a minimal profit than have an empty building. Write for a free booklet to : *Let's Go, English Tourist Board, Box X, P/C Hendon Road, Sunderland.*

1022   Holidays – working or training
Would you consider a working holiday which might even enable you to make a small profit on your vacation ? All sorts of work are covered : grape picking in France ; archaeological digs ; repairing canals and waterways ; maintaining and helping to run a narrow gauge railway in Wales ; carrying out repairs on a 16th century harbour – and many, many others. Or, if you are a student learning a European language, an exchange could be arranged with a student from that country who wishes to study English. These holidays are recommended for active people, aged 18–30, who do not think of a holiday merely as so many weeks of lying on the beach. For further information, read : *Working Holidays at Home and Abroad, Study Holidays at Home and Abroad, Sport and Adventure Holidays at Home and Abroad* or *School Travel and Exchange,* available from bookshops at 85p each – or direct from the publishers, *The Central Bureau of Educational Visits, 43 Dorset Street, London W1H 3FN* (send 85p plus 15p per book to cover postage and packing). Please note that the Bureau is *not* a job agency and does not give employment. But it will put you in contact with those who do. Three other useful reference books in this field, also available in bookshops, are : *Directory of Summer Jobs in*

Britain, Directory of Summer Jobs Abroad, and *Jobs and Careers Abroad,* all published by *Vacation Work Ltd., 9 Park End Street, Oxford (0865 41978).*

1023   Money for foreign holidays
The cheapest (but not the safest) way to take money abroad is to change all your holiday cash into foreign currency at a bank before going. But the rate of exchange may work against you if you bring any of it back home. Change your small coins into notes or buy something with them before starting home – British banks won't accept them.

1024   Railways – complaints
If you search your station, near the ticket office, you should find a poster with the address of your local Transport Users' Consultative Committee. Alternatively, write to : *The Central Committee, 3–4 Great Marlborough Street, London W1,* but only if your problem is a particular one, not just a general complaint about escalating fares.

1025   Train fares for commuters
If you commute to and from a city centre every working day, you do not need this book to tell you that an annual season ticket on BR is much cheaper than a daily ticket. But perhaps you have difficulty in finding the ready cash to buy a season ticket. If so, have you thought of asking your employer to advance the money and then deduct instalments from your pay packet? Many employers will do this. Alternatively, if you have a personal budget account with your bank, they will assist.

1026   Train travel (1)
Planning to make a longish (over £4 single) journey by train? By booking it at least 21 days ahead and by travelling on a Tuesday, Wednesday or Thursday, you can have the cost of your 2nd class return reduced to the price of a single.

1027   Train travel (2)
If you intend to make a one-day raid on London, a seaside resort or any other place of interest, book an Awayday ticket – it can save up to 35p in the £. There are also Awayday Special Bargains to specific places on which you can save even more.

1028   Train travel (3)

A Weekend Return ticket saves you up to 30p in the £ and is available – either 1st or 2nd Class – for most journeys over 75 miles. You travel on a Friday, Saturday or Sunday and return the same weekend.

1029   Train travel (4)

Journeys up to 75 miles are mostly covered by 17-Day Returns, which save up to 25p in the £. You can go on any day and return within 17 days – but if you travel out during Monday to Friday, you cannot return before the following Saturday. Ideal for holidays.

1030   Train travel – senior citizens

A Senior Citizen Railcard enables all those eligible (see final paragraph) to travel at a greatly reduced fare (half price for the year ending 31st March, 1977). There's a choice of two cards, one costing £3, the other £6, designed to suit different travel needs. The £3 Senior Citizen Awayday Card is for day trips and is half the cost of a normal, adult-price Awayday ticket (see no. 1027). As the latter is already a bargain offer, this concession is a saving on a saving, allowing day trips for only about one third of the full return fare.

The £6 Senior Citizen Railcard is for longer trips as well as days out. It enables the holder to buy ordinary single or return tickets and Awayday tickets at half the adult price.

To qualify for a Senior Citizen Railcard a person must (a) have held one in the previous year (the scheme began in 1976); (b) hold a retirement pension book or a retirement and supplementary pension book; (c) be over 60 and hold a Widow's Allowance, Pension or War Pension Order Book; (d) be over 65 (men) or 60 (women), living in the UK and receiving a retirement pension from overseas; or (e) be over 65 and living in the UK, even if not receiving a state retirement pension.

ACKNOWLEDGEMENTS

I would like to express my gratitude to the Readers' Service department of Mirror Group Newspapers for their assistance in verifying the accuracy of statements; to Mrs G. Mallard, tax consultant; to Mr J. R. Fernley of Swan Insurance Brokers; to Mr Alan Dobson of the BBC; to Mrs Hilda Houghton; and to my wife, Pat, for all the cookery and shopping experiments. My thanks are also due to Eastern Electricity, Eastern Gas, Leyland Paint & Wallpaper Ltd., *Which?* magazine, the National Westminster Bank Ltd., the Society of Herbalists, the Royal Automobile Club, the Automobile Association, the Solid Fuel Advisory Service, the Building Centre, the British Travel Association, the Estate Duty Office, the House Owners' Co-operative and the Watford Citizens' Advice Bureau.

NB: All prices, costs, fees, addresses and telephone numbers are correct at the time of going to press. Whilst every effort has been made to ensure that all the information in this book is correct, the reader is reminded that some areas (e.g. taxation) are subject to sudden changes in legislation.

TS